The Divine Declaration

*Ms Sue —
I wish for you, many many blessings. May your life unfold in ways greater than you ever imagined!*

*Jane —
3-31-06*

The Divine Declaration

Awaken to Your Divine Inner Power – Your Life Depends On It.

W. Jane Robinson

Infinite Endeavors

The Divine Declaration
Awaken To Your Divine Inner Power – Your Life Depends On It.

Copyright © 2006 by W. Jane Robinson
Published by: Infinite Endeavors Publishing Company, PO Box 1236, Oxford, GA 30054
U.S.A. http://www.thedivinedeclaration.com

All rights reserved. Printed in the United States of America. No part of this book may be reproduced by any mechanical, technical or audio process, transmitted or copied for public or private use – with the exception of "fair use" as brief quotations incorporated in articles and reviews without prior written permission of the publisher.

The author of this book does not directly or indirectly administer medical advice or prescribe the use of any technique as treatment for physical or medical issues. The author's and publisher's intent is only to offer information of a general nature to help you on your journey of emotional and spiritual development and well-being. The author and publisher assume no personal liability or any responsibility for your personal actions.

Kind Acknowledgements for Quotation Copyright Permissions:

Excerpt from *The Tibetan Book of Living and Dying* by Sogyal Rinpoche © 1993 by Rigpa Fellowship. Used by permission of HarperCollins Publishers.
Excerpt from *A Return to Love* by Marianne Williamson © 1992 by Marianne Williamson. Used by permission of HarperCollins Publishers.
Excerpt from *The Science of Mind* by Ernest Holmes © 1938 by Ernest Holmes. Used by permission of the Ernest Holmes Institute/Science of Mind.
Excerpt from *Light Emerging* by Barbara Ann Brennan, © 1993 by Barbara Ann Brennan. Used by permission of Bantam Books, a division of Random House, Inc.
Excerpt from *Illusions: The Adventures of A Reluctant Messiah* by Richard Bach © 1977 by Richard Bach and Leslie Parrish-Bach. Used by permission of Dell Publishing, a division of Random House, Inc.
Excerpt from *Creative Visualization* by Shakti Gawain ©2002, 1995, 1978 by Shakti Gawain. Used by permission of New World Library.
Excerpt from 'Mind/Body Connection: How Your Emotions Affect Your Health.' Reproduced with permission from 'Mind/Body Connection: How Your Emotions Affect Your Health,' February 2004, *http://familydoctor.org/782.xml*. Copyright © 2004 American Academy of Family Physicians. All Rights Reserved.
Excerpt from "Longevity May Have Spiritual Link" by Paula J. Wart, Vanderbilt University, Health Plus Wellness Program © 2001. Used by permission of Paula J. Wart.

Publisher's Cataloging-in-Publication Data

Robinson, W. Jane.
 The divine declaration : awaken to your divine inner power--your life depends on it / W. Jane Robinson. – 1st ed.
 p. cm.
 Includes bibliographical references.
 LCCN 2005903749
 ISBN 0-9760921-0-7 (Trade paper)
 ISBN 0-9760921-7-4 (Hardcover)

 1. Self-actualization (Psychology) 2. Spirituality.
 3. Conduct of life. 4. Spiritual healing. I. Title.

BF637.S4R63 2006   158.1
          QBI05-700180

Cover Design by George Foster
Interior Design by Cheryl L. Cromer – Square Moon Custom Publishing, Inc.
Edited by Kim Chimene and Hal Zina Bennett
Copy Edited by Adele Brinkley

Contents

Acknowledgements viii

Introduction xi

Part I: Facts About Your Divine Inner Power: How and Why Your Divine Inner Power Connection Impacts Your Life. 1

   Chapter One: Your Divine Inner Power 3

      Identify Your Divine Inner Power
      Understand the Power Inside You
      The Importance of This Power in Your Life
      A Divine Declaration. 24

   Chapter Two: Resistance to Your Divine Inner Power:
   Fear, Low Self-Esteem and Old Negative Programming . . . 27

      Examine Three Major Challenges in Awakening to Your
        Divine Inner Power
      Clearing Fear, Low Self-Esteem and Old Negative
        Programming
      A Divine Declaration. 52

Part II: Examine the Power of Your Thoughts: How Your Thoughts Create Your Life Experience 55

   Chapter Three: How Your Thoughts Affect Your Life 57

      How to Change Your Thoughts and Create What You Want
        in Your Life
      Planting and Growing Seeds of Success
      Exercising Your Divine Inner Power and Positive Thinking
      Affirmations of Knowing
      A Divine Declaration. 72

   Chapter Four: The Mind/Body/Spirit Connection 75

      Understanding This Connection

    Increase Your Well-Being
    Meditation and Prayer as it Relates to Your Well-Being
    Integrative Healing
    Youthing
    A Divine Declaration........................... 92

Part III: Experience and Expand Your Divine Inner Power: How to Awaken To, Experience, and Expand Your Divine Inner Power 95

    Chapter Five: How to Awaken To, Experience, and Expand Your Divine Inner Power........................ 97

        Meditation
        Affirmative Prayer
        Creative Visualization
        Treasure Mapping
        Journaling
        A Divine Declaration........................... 120

    Chapter Six: Your Support System 123

        Surround Yourself With Supportive People
        Your Internal Support System
        Internal Locus of Control and Resilience
        A Divine Declaration........................... 134

    Chapter Seven: Love, Gratitude, and Forgiveness 137

        Why and How Love, Gratitude and Forgiveness Are Vital in Awakening to Your Divine Inner Power
        Learn to Love Your*Self*, Experience Gratitude, and Forgiveness
        A Divine Declaration........................... 152

Part IV: Live in Connection With Your Divine Inner Power: How to Live in Connection With Your Divine Inner Power 155

    Chapter Eight: Your Divine Right Livelihood 157

Discovering Your Divine Right Livelihood
Follow Your Dreams and Take Action in the Direction of
  Your Dreams
A Divine Declaration............................. 168

Chapter Nine: Opening to the Flow of the Universe
  and Sharing 171

  The Cycle of Universal Flow
  Allow the Divine Flow of the Universe to Support You
  The Value of Sharing and Helping Others
  A Divine Declaration 184

**Part V: Stand Tall and Experience a Life of Divine Inner Power:
How to Reinforce, Stand Tall, and Enjoy the Rewards of Your
Divine Inner Power Connection** 187

  Chapter Ten: Reinforcement Tools for Connecting With Your
    Divine Inner Power 189

    External Tools Available to Help You Awaken to Your Divine
      Connection and Take Back Your Power
    A Divine Declaration.......................... 202

  Chapter Eleven: Stand Tall, Live Authentically, Set Personal
    Boundaries, and Enjoy Living in Your Divine Inner
    Power 205

    Stand Tall — Your Non-Verbal Language Reveals Your Inner
      Belief System
    Live Authentically
    Setting Boundaries — Professional, Emotional, and Spiritual
    You Deserve Happiness and Success
    A Divine Declaration.......................... 218

  Chapter Twelve: The Divine Declaration................ 221
Bibliography & Recommended Reading 233

Acknowledgements

I would like to express my sincere appreciation to everyone who has helped me on my journey. I am grateful each and every day for my foster families who have embraced me as one of their own: the Dodson Family, the LeJeune Family and the Leonard Family. I am also very grateful for my brothers and sisters and their wonderful families who support me and share their lives with me. It is with heartfelt love that I thank my precious pups, Pooh and Panda, and my foster mom's precious pups, Tinkerbell and Beau, who have brought a beautiful dimension to my life. I express my humble gratitude to the spiritual, mental, and physical mentors who have helped me in so many ways: Dr. Michele Aguayo, Rebecca Boyd, Susan Martin, Betty Shamblin, Mr. Watkins, and Joe Whitwell. Thank you to my wonderful friends who have left an indelible impression on my life: Kim and Mark Chimene, Leslie Gutherie, and Traci Davis. I sincerely appreciate my friends and co-workers who have helped bring this book to life: Kim Chimene, Cheryl Cromer, and Heidi Rizzi. Thank you, Hal Zina Bennett for your writing direction and supportive comments, George Foster for the great cover design, and Adele Brinkley for copy editing this book. Thank you all for your contribution to my life journey!

Acknowledgements

I dedicate this book to…

*Harry and Dyanne Dodson who have helped anchor my life.
My "Mom," Pat LeJeune, my spiritual mother and friend
who is my greatest fan and always inspires me to be my best.
My foster father Orval LeJeune, I am proud
to be one of his daughters.
Our four precious pups Pooh, Panda, Tinkerbell
and Beau, thank you for being our furry angels.*

*In loving memory of Catherine and Earl Leonard, my first
foster parents, without whose love and caring this book
and my life would be much less.*

I love you all beyond words.

Introduction

A pervasive longing for a deeper connection, experienced by millions of us, is a driving force in life. Few of us escape the feelings of abandonment, unworthiness, and hopelessness at the heart of this longing. We turn to books, seminars, education, religion, and even to addictive behaviors, to either dull our pain and longing or uncover our sense of self-worth, belonging, and lovability that we somehow know is our birthright.

What if you were given a document, a declaration to provide you direction that also reveals how to reclaim your Divine Inner Power, satisfy your longing, and reunite you with infinite love?

The Divine Declaration is here to serve as your creed to help you reclaim you personal power, support you on your life path, and reinforce your divine connection. *The Divine Declaration* provides you a solid document of hope and healing. It is the foundational step forward on a magnificent life journey.

Awakening to our true divine nature is our greatest journey. This inner journey unlocks the door to our dreams and fulfillment, and also clears the path for our personal power and growth. It yields fertile ground for us to plant our life's dreams and to participate as we grow in the direction of these dreams. During encounters with life's adversities, our Divine Inner Power is the internal strength to help us through these challenges.

The Divine Declaration

I embarked on this inner journey twenty years ago, pursuing and nurturing this inner awakening with fervency and dedication, sometimes wishing I had encountered this knowledge much earlier in my life.

I was placed in the state foster care system as a toddler and remained in foster care until I "aged out" at eighteen. In adulthood I diligently sought, and eventually discovered, how to heal my emotional wounds and ultimately establish a sense of stability, love, and connection.

The Divine Declaration offers a unique perspective on the longing that reaches deeply into our sense of worthiness and our ability to love and be loved. In this book, I candidly share with you an effective healing system I have utilized to overcome wounds of abandonment, disconnection from biological parents, and the emotional indifference of some of my early caregivers. The insights and tools revealed in *The Divine Declaration* will ultimately open new doors to a deeply satisfying life.

I bring you *The Divine Declaration* as an easy-to-follow roadmap for negotiating the path to the divine power residing within each of us. Whether you were raised in a stable home with two caring parents, or in the chaotic shuffle through foster homes, the journey you will take in this book is invaluable. The guidance relating to openly affirming our spiritual connection and personal power makes *The Divine Declaration* a key resource for unlocking and healing the years of intense, often hidden, emotional pain at the heart of one of humanity's most universal wounds.

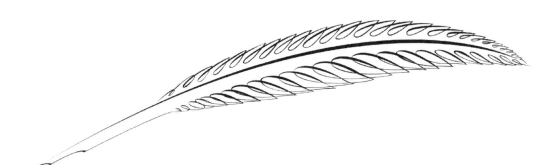

Section One

Facts About Your Divine Inner Power

Chapter One

Your Divine Inner Power

The Divine Declaration

To truely know oneself

"Most powerful is he who has himself in his own power."

— *Seneca*

Your Divine Inner Power

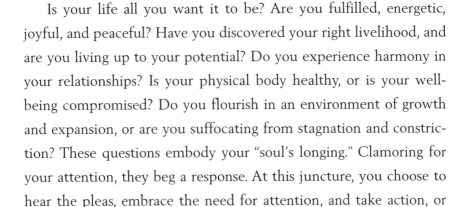

Is your life all you want it to be? Are you fulfilled, energetic, joyful, and peaceful? Have you discovered your right livelihood, and are you living up to your potential? Do you experience harmony in your relationships? Is your physical body healthy, or is your well-being compromised? Do you flourish in an environment of growth and expansion, or are you suffocating from stagnation and constriction? These questions embody your "soul's longing." Clamoring for your attention, they beg a response. At this juncture, you choose to hear the pleas, embrace the need for attention, and take action, or you turn your back on your deepest desires, close the door, and walk away. You decide between living fully and merely existing.

Each of us has our own unique hopes and dreams. We want to enjoy greater peace and joy and would benefit from spiritual, emotional, and physical harmony. But in the grueling get-ahead-at-all-costs race, many people lose hope, bury their dreams, and experience disharmony in their relationships and physical health. We speed through the day, multi-tasking, with no time to recall how critical the role of our life's hopes and dreams. It is hazardous to our physical, mental, emotional, and spiritual well-being to race through life chasing the next thrill or material possession, greeting the grim reapers of emptiness and despair on the heels of each conquest.

Many people balance their lives on the tightrope of repressed emotions, disconnected from their Divine Inner Power [Holy Spirit]. Suspended on the high wire of quiet desperation, they are gripped by fear. They have relinquished their inner power to a job, a partner, a way of life, or to something external and disconnected from themselves.

To free your life from this desperation and take back your power, awaken to and connect with your Divine Inner Power [Holy Spirit]. Your Divine Inner Power is the power inside you — the power of you that is connected to God or the Divine Source of the universe. It is the eternal, magnificent creative force in your life, and it is awaiting your awakening.

We must take this path of inner exploration if we are to awaken to our divine nature, take back our power, create more harmony, and fulfill our dreams. Through this connection and understanding, we realize we are more than our physical bodies — we are an expression of the divine. We are spiritual beings experiencing life through our physical expressions. [Spirit, soul and body]

When we connect with our Divine Inner Power, we regain hope and zest for life. We experience this connection as a harmonious relationship with ourselves. From this place of internal peace, we are able to reach out and extend this harmony to our fellow travelers.

This book offers you guidance and hope for your journey. It is by way of your inner examination and connecting with your Divine

[margin note: Finding God's will in your life]

Your Divine Inner Power

[Margin note above title: "A child of God, covered w/ Grace"]

Inner Power that you discover the gem of who you really are. I will provide you with encouragement and direction in awakening to and connecting with your Divine *Self*, the real you. You will discover great joy, peace, and spiritual, emotional, and physical balance. The techniques in this book and The Divine Declaration at the close of each chapter will help you accelerate your personal and spiritual growth.

Open your heart and mind to the possibility of fulfilling your life's dreams. The life you desire is within your reach, waiting only for you to declare your divine heritage. You are a divine emanation of God, and you have a power inside that is connected to God, despite any physical circumstances.

[Margin note: "This happens once you acept his Son Jesus as your savior"]

These powerful truths are awaiting your awakening at this very moment. You can have a life of joy and abundance through awakening to your Divine Inner Power. Do you believe this? Or, do you say to yourself, "Oh, not me. I have made many mistakes, and I am not worthy. My dream is out of reach. I wouldn't even know where to start. I really want to be happy, but I am afraid of how my life will change if I awaken to my divinity and connect with my inner power."

[Left margin note: "For by GRACE are ye saved..."]

Through this book, you will discover awakening is a powerful journey, and that you can create the life you desire. You will also challenge fear and enjoy the happiness you wish for as you pursue this path. When you embark on this inner journey, you will truly discover an amazing new world.

[Right margin note: "Trust the Lord w/all your heart and lean not until your own understandings"]

The Divine Declaration

THE POWER

How do we recognize this divine universal power revered as God by Christians, Brahma by Hindus, Buddha by Buddhists, or by others as the Is, the Creative Energy, the One, or the Source? This power is the unlimited and compelling force that drives us to make great things happen. *["I am" the way, the truth + the light, no man cometh unto the father but by me..]*

As we look around, we easily enjoy the abundance in the starry heaven, a bright sunny day, a soothing rain, a sunset on the ocean's horizon, vast mountain ranges, a blooming flower, a mighty oak tree or a big blue sky. The same power creating beauty and abundance is the ONE energy at the center of our beating hearts and life breath, the love of a pet, the connection with our loved ones, and the feelings of accomplishment. It is the intuition *[JESUS]* something is right.

As you connect with this power, you may utilize the effective method of FEELS Powerful Living in this book as a map or guide for your inner journey. It serves as a strategic process for declaring, awakening to, and connecting with your Divine Inner Power. As we FEEL *[the Holy Spirit guides us]* our power, we recognize our infinite nature because consciously awakening to our Divine Inner Power, combined with feeling our power and connection, is vital to how we experience our world. FEELS Powerful Living includes the following steps:

Facts about your Divine Inner Power – Learn how and why this connection impacts your life.

Examine the power of your thoughts.

Experience and expand your Divine Inner Power.

Live in connection with your Divine Inner Power.

Stand tall and experience a life of Divine Inner Power.

Your Divine Inner Power

Marianne Williamson wrote eloquently of our Divine Inner Power in her book *A Return to Love* —

Our deepest fear is not that we are inadequate. Our deepest fear is that we are powerful beyond measure. It is our light, not our darkness, that most frightens us. We ask ourselves, who am I to be brilliant, gorgeous, talented, and fabulous? Actually, <u>who are you not to be</u>? You are a child of God. Your playing small doesn't serve the world. There is nothing enlightened about shrinking so that other people won't feel insecure around you. We were all meant to shine, as children do. We were born to make manifest the glory of God within us. <u>It is not just in some of us; it is in everyone</u>. And, as we let our own light shine, we unconsciously give other people permission to do the same. As we are liberated from our own fear, our presence automatically liberates others.

My initiation into the magnificent use of this divine power was revealed when I contacted a counselor to work on relationship issues and career challenges I faced. My counselor said, "You need to take your power back."

I thought, "What is she saying?" She certainly wasn't stroking my ego or humoring me to soothe my desperation with "take your power back." After all, I thought I was somewhat powerful, so I felt a little smug.

"What do you mean take my power back?" I asked, dangling between desperation and determination. I was upset about the relationship and my unfulfilled career, but at least I felt conscious of my inner power. We continued working on my issues together, and over the years, I have slowly and steadfastly taken back my power and learned valuable tools for embracing my divine connection to the divine universal power.

[Margin note: God has a plan in his will for each one of us...]

The Divine Declaration

Embracing my Divine Inner Power has changed my life. What a transformation I've made from the frightened young girl I was to a woman with the confidence to pursue my goals. It has been a journey of enlightenment and labor. I have survived a divorce, completed a degree, changed career paths, bought a home, and adopted two precious puppies — a Shih-Tzu named Pooh and a Shih-Tzu/Jack Russell mix named Panda (an unbelievable joy but a new level of responsibility for me). Now I am fervently pursuing the rest of my dreams.

Working consciously with my inner power has been liberating. Although I certainly didn't fully understand this power when the counselor instructed me to "take control of my power," looking back I see that I had used it as a tool for surviving my childhood. I had a strong determination, even as child, but it proved an even more useful tool when I consciously understood the power.

[True] When we encounter joyful people who have followed their dreams and created the life they desire, we wonder about the source of their power. It is a power greater than the physical realm. These are people who have connected with their Divine Inner Power, who live in their divinity, make great contributions, and who watch the world unfold as an exciting and abundant place. *[God's Grace]* *[Plant your seed, where the rain is falling...]*

In his book *Illusions*, Richard Bach compares a movie projector to our imagination with the film as the information we feed into our imagination. Translate this concept and view the projector as your belief system of who you are and the film as the frames of information you allow to mold that system. People who choose to live their dreams and move beyond the status quo allow a film of the life they'd

Your Divine Inner Power

dreamed to run through their projector. They are unwilling to sit back and view a film someone else fed into the projector or to be forced to watch the same film everyone else is watching.

As I write this book and project the information on the screen of my life, I am living my dream and utilizing this universal power. At times, I am connected and feel the information flow through my fingers onto the blank page with ease. My hope is that you allow the information in this book to impose an image on a frame in your film, and view yourself following your dreams as you release your own creation through connection with your Divine Inner Power.

The great spiritual masters openly believed in their divine connection and power. They eagerly shared their message of divine connection with us. Jesus, Buddha, and Gandhi, to name a few, have impacted the world with their divinity. We witness the contributions of these spiritual masters through their enlightening and loving spiritual teachings.

In his teachings, Jesus clearly stated his belief in our divine connection through this powerful message found in John 14:10-12 —

> [10] Believest thou not that I am the Father, and the Father in me? the words that I speak unto you I speak not of myself: but the Father that dwelleth in me, he doeth the works.
>
> [11] Believe me that I am in the Father, and the Father in me: or else believe me for the very works sake.
>
> [12] Verily, verily, I say unto you, He that believeth on me, the works that I do he shall do also; and greater works than these shall he do; because I go unto my Father.

The Divine Declaration

Jesus not only stated that he could perform these works through his connection with God, but that it was also possible for those who believe in their connection with God to perform even greater works.

Buddha spoke of our ordinary nature and of our true nature. The ordinary nature to which he refers is connected to the physical realm and experiences the unpleasant things in life such as fear and suffering. Our true nature is the wise, pure, and perfect part of our being, the divine part of us or the Buddha nature. According to Buddha's teachings, the only variance between an ordinary person and an enlightened Buddha is that the ordinary person has not yet awakened to his or her true divine nature.

Mahatma Gandhi, a great master of spirituality and compassion, also shared his view of our divinity. In his *Selected Letters, Part One*, he wrote, "In working out plans of self-restraint, attention must not for a moment be withdrawn from the fact that we are all sparks of the divine and therefore partake of its nature…."

Many great spiritual masters are known throughout the world, but there are also masters all around us, each one connected to his or her divinity, inspiring and leading us to look inside and awaken to our divinity. Various individuals, perhaps unrecognized worldwide, have illuminated our lives in important ways. If you stop and consider it, you will recognize there are people you know who have also looked inside to discover the jewel of their divinity. They recognized their inner power and polished their inner awareness, clearing away the debris in order to reveal their bright light. They may not have spoken directly about your divinity, but they touched your life in some way that helped you to live up to your potential.

Your Divine Inner Power

[Margin note: We must live in the spirit, not the Flesh]

Without understanding and connecting to this inner power, we flounder, desperately arranging life events in the physical realm and seeking distraction from emotional pain. We gaze up the corporate ladder, buy new toys — cars, houses, second homes, trips, electronic gadgets, and various other items to fill the void. We also seek activities in an effort to escape the boredom of mundane work and life, but at the end of the day, we still feel empty. Focusing on the physical plane by accumulating things or filling our minds constantly with events in an effort to fulfill the spiritual void, is an empty endeavor. Through connecting with our Divine Inner Power and tapping into our divinity, we are able to manifest and enjoy the abundance we create in our physical lives.

You may ask, "What about the people who have material wealth, but who are unkind and totally out of touch with their divine power? They are stealing, cheating, lying, and not at all living in a space of divinity. Why do they have abundance?"

You would be right to wonder about these people. They may have wealth and abundance in the physical plane, but are they really happy inside, or are they simply caught up in their own chase? Without the divine connection, *[Margin note: Jesus leading the way]* a spiritual void remains, leaving them to pursue the next material possession as an analgesic for the pain.

In his book, *The Tibetan Book of Living and Dying*, Sogyal Rinpoche conveys poignantly the emptiness of this chase and the value of non-attachment to the physical realm. He tells us that we are afraid of death because we really have no idea of who we are. We are disconnected from our divinity and inner power and we are

The Divine Declaration

attached to our identity that "depends entirely on an endless collection of things to prop it up: our name, our 'biography,' our partners, family, home, friends, credit cards…It is on their fragile and transient support that we rely for our security. So when they are all taken away, will we have any idea of who we really are?"

However, when we connect with our inherent divinity, we are filled by divine power and positioned to attract our greatest good. Because like attracts like, we attract what we believe we deserve and what we are inside. We attract into our lives elements that are in sync with us. If we are in a healthy space, we attract healthy relationships and dynamics into our life. Conversely, if we are needy and unhealthy, we attract people and things of like manner.

It is important to understand this power is available for everyone. It does not discriminate. Divine Source knows only a loving nature, and, like the sun, shines for everyone. We must decide to face the light if we are to connect to the divine energy. The God energy of the universe is in and around everything. It is the cord that runs through all, connecting us as ONE. While we are each a unique aspect of this ONE energy, the energy is universal at the origination point.

I gained insight into this indiscriminate ONE energy concept through personal experience. Growing up in several foster homes left me with the grand illusion that anyone who enjoyed the benefits of a childhood with his or her natural parents is emotionally healthy. I thought people who grew up with their biological parents were entitled to divine power, and I was somehow left out. The illusion has since been shattered. I now understand that some of these people, even with their natural parents, faced their own adversities and struggled to recognize or embrace their Divine Inner Power. Not recognizing this power leaves us at the mercy of others — a victim. *One must first forgive all – including self...*

Now I know Divine Inner Power is available to all who open to this magnificent energy. Similar to electricity, the current is equally available to anyone who turns on the switch. We each choose to illuminate the room or to remain in the dark.

It is our reaction to a situation that affects our reality, not the circumstances of the situation. When we recognize and connect with *→ allow Jesus to work* this power, we develop greater control of our reactions. Without knowing this power, we are rudderless and subject to outside forces over which we have no control.

Deciding to turn on our inner light opens the connection to our Divine Inner Power and enables us to accomplish great things. We will often find ourselves saying, "Wow, I did that!"

Allowing Jesus to lead the way
Connecting with our power leads us to our higher *Self* and our *His light* life's path. As we walk our path, the light of our Divine Inner Power illuminates our way. If we stumble, we have a lighted path and we are better able to regain our footing and step forward on our journey.

This power has also served me in changing careers from accounting and management to sales and to my dream of being a writer. I have <u>embraced</u> this inner connection, and it has supported me on my journey. The light pours through abundantly when I return to my center *God*, remember who I am, and connect with my divine nature.

The Divine Declaration

Divine Inner Power leads us to fulfillment in the spiritual, emotional, and physical realm. It sustains us during challenging times and harbors our tranquility. Storms may roll through, but we now have the shelter of our inner power as a safe harbor. We can trim our sails as we set our course and use the force of our Divine Inner Power to reach our destination. Understanding our true nature protects us from being blown around by damaging winds and soaked by pounding rains that dampen our spirits. [Trials]

The divine force is also similar to a radio wave. You can tune into any station you like. If it is not satisfying, turn the dial and tune into another station more in concert with your energy [Christ like]. The waves already exist, you simply tune into what works for you. If you have selected a station in the past that isn't working for you now, you are not required to remain at that position. Tune your life to another frequency. It is your choice. You control the dial.

When we start our automobiles, switch on a light or computer, or plant a garden, we may not have a complete understanding of how all of the components work together to make these things happen, but we trust the car will start, the light will turn on, the computer will work, and the garden will grow. We need this trust in order to know our Divine Inner Power will help us on our journey and lead us to our highest good. It's not a blind faith, but a knowing that this divine connection brings power into our lives. It is a law of the universe — a divine declaration. [God only responds thru Jesus Christ only]

Believing in our own inner power and focusing on the creation of our dreams takes us in the direction of our dominant thoughts. Thoughts are like a blueprint for a house. Without the blueprint,

[margin note: It is only done by faith..]

chaos reigns, and the end result may be entirely different than what we intended to build. If you spend time focusing on what you really want in life and if it doesn't displace another person's highest good, your dream is anchored on a firm foundation.

For example, as I continued connecting to my inner power, I moved forward with writing this book. <u>Writing and helping others live their dreams are important missions for me</u>. I have worked to press through my fears of failure. The seed for this book germinated for approximately one year. During the next year, I dabbled at writing it, apprehensive of the outcome. Would it be what I wanted it to be? Would I be a successful writer? I finally decided if I continued with this kind of "testing the waters" behavior, I might never live my dreams. So I took to the task of completing the book rather than concerning myself with the outcome. Knowing with certainty this was the direction I wanted to take, I dove into the deep end. I felt the refreshing supporting waters surround me as I resurfaced, invigorated from the plunge of diving into my own sea of dreams.

I have achieved success through careers in sales and accounting, but writing and helping others through my writing has remained my dream. Because of the importance of this dream, I was cautious. I have been pleasantly surprised by <u>confirming signs along the way</u>. → Highly important *[margin note: In the word of God]*

Getting this book into print seemed to take on a life of its own. I found support through friends and family during the creation process. Initially, their beliefs in my work were greater than my own. They continued cheering me on through my bouts of trepidation. The book developed, and as I worked through releasing the fear, I

The Divine Declaration

found it easier to write. I garnered more enthusiasm as I completed each chapter.

Do you remember the children's book, *The Little Engine That Could*? When things seemed scary and impossible, the little engine embraced his inner power, continued his belief, and affirmed that he could do the job. And he did! This is the type of journey I invite you to take with me. You can make it up the hill and reach your dreams too.

Having grown up as a child in the foster care system, I was the little engine that could. I will always remember the emotional mountains I climbed.* You have likely climbed your own mountains as well.

My childhood abandonment issue was a challenging terrain. After my father passed away, I was taken from my mother because of her alcoholism. Sometimes I stumbled on the ascending path. The devastating blow occurred at age seven when I had to leave my first foster home. Leaving my foster family choked off my steam. I was heartbroken. Emotionally, I thought of my foster parents as my mom and dad. My foster mother had diabetes and her failing health required my sister and me to move to a different home where my older brother and sister lived.

While I was glad to be reunited with my siblings, the new foster home was sterile and unfeeling. We were not allowed to see my original foster parents for more than a year. I was sick at school and muddled through the days, finding my way to the clinic almost every day. "Why didn't my first foster family want to see me?" I often asked myself.

Your Divine Inner Power

As it happened, and with a bit of synchronicity, we encountered my first foster family at a department store and discovered they had been trying to get in touch with us since we had left their home. The new foster mother and the social worker blocked the contact because they did not think it was a good idea for us to continue our relationship. They had decided it would upset us to keep the contact if we could not live with them.

This chance meeting changed everything. I remember my original foster mother calling weekly to ask if we could visit her for the weekend. She was diligent even with her failing health. Eventually, I stayed weekends with her daughter (my foster sister) and her family. I experienced a loving environment and great adventure with them. We enjoyed my nephews' little league baseball games, adventurous rides in the dune-buggy or go-cart, and swimming in their pool. I enjoyed my time with them and <u>felt a natural love</u>. It was a great escape from my home environment during the week.

My older brother and sisters also allowed my siblings and me to visit their homes for weekends and week-long stays during the summer. The time spent with my original foster family and my siblings was a much-needed reprieve that helped save me from emotionally tumbling down the mountain.

I eagerly anticipated those weekends and focused on school and my friends during the week. This arrangement continued until I was fourteen and life for me at the second foster home became unbearable. I then moved to another temporary foster home for one year.

While at this home, I met a new friend at school. I began staying weekends with her family. They were sophisticated and generous, and I enjoyed spending time with them. After many weekends with them and some tactical work from my friend and her parents with Family and Children Services, they opened their home to me. On my sixteenth birthday, I moved in with my new foster family. I was elated to be with them and lived with them until I married. They were then, and continue to be, great parents to me.

The love of my first foster family, my natural brothers and sisters who took the time to care about me, the devotion and love of my new foster family, and good friends all helped my efforts to maintain enough strength and persevere on the strenuous climb to emotional maturity.

Although some of my childhood experiences were dark and scary, I had many blessings for which I am very grateful. I consider my first and last foster families true families. They inspired and supported me while I huffed and puffed up the mountain to find my inner power and divine connection. My natural brothers and sisters also inspired and supported me — a definite bonus. Ultimately, I knew it was my responsibility to create the life I desired. I had to awaken to and connect with my Divine Inner Power.

Yes, this power is like the sun and shines for us all, but we also need to be aware that we may encounter people who opt to stand in the shadow. Either consciously or by default, they turn their backs to the light. The shadow of the people who remain in the dark affects everyone and everything around them. Lacking recognition of their Divine Inner Power results in negativity, dampens hope, and diminishes the light of creativity and purpose. Any negative reinforcements we received in childhood were most likely cast upon us by those who were out of touch with their divine power.

As a child, I encountered people who supported me and people who were callous and indifferent to my needs. Callousness and indifference are characteristics of people I refer to as "shadow people." Shadow people are disconnected from their own divinity and inner power. Because they are out of touch with their own divine nature, they are unable to reach out and support others on their journey. Spending time with these people dims our own light. Our energy is channeled into desperately warding off their negative energy. This lower energy relates to survival and is basic in nature. A person operating in lower energy typically functions from fear and strives to survive through desperate means.

Challenging relationships are not limited to our familial relationships. You can observe lower level energy in various environments.

Perhaps you, like me, have found yourself in low energy environments at work. Employees in survival mode often seem angry and project these feelings onto others in the office. Some are in fear of never getting enough prestige or money to fill their inner void; therefore, they take negative measures to ward off fears of emotional or monetary poverty.

In work environments, I've observed people who weren't able to speak to others in the office because they were so unhappy, employees embezzling from the company and who were eventually caught, others who encroached on personal and professional boundaries, those involved in numerous office romances, and others whose attitudes were, "look who I know, how smart I am, and at what I've done."

The Divine Declaration

We all know how challenging it can be to interact with people who usurp your positive energy with their negativity.

While the pain and devastation from the past may cast a cold shadow on life, we may choose at any time to face the light and move beyond merely surviving to living fully. My own issues of abandonment and feeling not quite "good enough" because my biological mother released me into foster care, coupled with the experience in two of my foster homes, were my nemesis for many years.

Through the process in this book, I will help you avoid the crushing stampede of negative programming and provide you guidance to connect with your Divine Inner Power. You, too, can step into the light any time you choose and feel the warm rays of your divine inheritance. Through the inner journey I share with you in this book, it is my hope that you will lighten up, shine, and declare your Divine Inner Power.

Ask yourself now: Am I truly happy? Am I living the life I really want to live? Am I at peace? Am I healthy? Am I living in abundance and joy? Am I learning through ease and grace?

If you answered *yes* to any of these questions, you are on your way to awakening to this inner power. Great! The chapters ahead will provide grounded support of your divinity and help you soar even higher on your journey. However, if you answered *no* to any or all of these questions, take heart. This book will provide you guidance as you you reach inside and free your Divine Inner Power.

Take your belief system to a new level, enjoy the process in this book and feel, see, hear, and know this new world as it opens to you.

Your Divine Inner Power

This is a book of action and awakening, and of reaping the rewards you desire for your life. Enjoy your journey and know it is now your turn to declare your divinity, connect with the infinite flow of your Divine Inner Power, take back your power, and claim your divine inheritance.

The Divine Declaration

The Divine Declaration 1 – Understanding My Divinity and Power

When in the course of my life, I find repression, unhappiness, ill-health, a chaotic state of mind, and a general sense of hopelessness, it is essential that I release any old programming, ties to the past, current situations, or people who are not supportive of my happiness, my ability to pursue my dreams, my general well-being, and my spiritual, emotional, and mental growth. I now assume my connection to God, the Divine Source, and recognize the power residing inside of me. I was created by the Divine Source; therefore, it must hold true that I am connected to this divinity and have access to a greater power. It is inside of me. It is my divine inheritance. I choose a new path of freedom from the albatross of unworthiness today. The weight is gone. A new world awaits me. And, so it is.

Thank you, Universe. Thank you, God.

Your Divine Inner Power

I now accept as true and hold these truths to be evident: I am a divine being, a spark of the Divine Source. I am worthy. I am loving and loved. I live in a supportive world, supported by God, the Divine Source. My inheritance is abundance in love, health, joy, peace, and all my heart's desires for a wonderful life. I know that I deserve the best in life, and it is mine. All I need to do is to awaken to this truth. My divine power is available anytime I choose to use it. It is always there and serves as a beacon guiding me on the path of my highest good. I fulfill my dreams and live in the abundance and joy that it is mine. My life is a work in progress. I am on my path of love and light. I am excited about the future, able to let go of the past and find peace in the present moment. With great fortitude, I embark on this journey of light. My divine connection is infinite, and my divine power is unlimited. I can soar. I have the ability to make my dreams come true.

Today, I declare my divinity and access my power with courage and commitment.

This is my Divine Declaration.

Chapter Two

Resistance to Your Divine Inner Power: Fear, Low Self-Esteem, Old Negative Programming

The Divine Declaration

"Up to a point a man's life is shaped by environment, heredity, and movements and changes in the world about him. Then there comes a time when it lies within his grasp to shape the clay of his life into the sort of thing he wishes to be. Only the weak blame parents, their race, their times, lack of good fortune, or the quirks of fate. Everyone has it within his power to say, 'This I am today; that I will be tomorrow.'"

— Louis L'Amour

Resistance to Your Divine Inner Power

Resistance is a common response to change. Often we find many hurdles to clear in connecting with our Divine Inner Power. Some of our most powerful resistance is founded in fear, low self-esteem, and old negative programming, coupled with empirical identification to past experiences. You may need to pole vault these hurdles in the process of connecting with your Divine Inner Power, but you can clear them.

Ponder this: Have you ever been afraid of either failing or succeeding? Fear of either is an emotional scavenger delaying your dreams and waiting to devour your inner power. It is difficult to discern between the two, because fear of either success or failure can be paralyzing. However, once again, you can overcome this obstacle on your way to living in your power.

Low self-esteem plagues our society, and like a sponge, soaks up our hope and self-love. Your self-esteem is how you feel about you. Self-esteem is not the ego. It is the true love and value of who you are. The ego is a part of our personality that requires outer stroking. If your self-esteem is damaged, you may not feel you can have the life you really want — or that you even deserve it. Without a healthy sense of self-worth, we live in perpetual fear and anxiety. We accept a life that falls short of our dreams. We simply do not feel we deserve any more. Thus, we settle for less and wonder why we didn't receive something greater.

Old negative programming wields its power by feeding our fears and destroying our self-esteem. It permeates the subconscious mind, forming negative thought patterns, which erode our personal value. Old negative programming takes various forms. We may have absorbed negative emotional constructs connected to our identity from outright verbal abuse, or from subtle sources, such as how we were treated as children.

For example, I worked on a particular negative program in my life for many years. The program played over in my mind: I must not be as good as other people; therefore, others are more important than me, and their needs and desires are also more important.

This belief was instilled in my psyche as a child. No one ever told me I was unimportant, but nonetheless my life as a foster child perpetuated the belief. In one of my foster homes, the guardian treated us (the foster children) with indifference and lavished her own grandchildren with love, affection, and special favors. We did not celebrate our birthdays, but were taken to the grandchildren's birthday parties. We were not allowed certain foods, but when her grandchildren visited they were allowed to eat our forbidden foods. We weren't allowed to open the refrigerator, and the freezer was under lock and key.

While these events may not be considered flagrant abuse, they certainly shaped how my siblings and I viewed our rights. We were confused about our sense of belonging and value in relationship to other people who were loved by their biological family.

After working diligently on this issue, I reached the awareness we were innocent children and the foster parent was <u>projecting her own inability to care for others onto us</u>. I now recognize when I replay the tape and consciously move my thoughts to my true nature. I simply erase the foster parent's issues around my identity. Sometimes I visualize myself erasing a chalk board and rewriting my script.

Old, negative programming issues may have been imparted verbally by a parent, authority figure, or peer. For example, an authority figure repetitively stating to a child, "You are lazy and dumb, and you will not amount to anything when you grow up," is devastating. You may have experienced your own form of old, negative programming, and these words or programs remain obstacles on your path to fulfillment.

Let's explore each of these areas of resistance and examine their relationship to your declaring and connecting with your Divine Inner Power.

FEAR

Fear is an incredibly powerful barrier to connecting with our Divine Inner Power. It blocks momentum and creativity, and prevents us from living our dreams and connecting with our inner power. We fear success, failure, death, living, losing a job or relationship, staying in a bad job or relationship, changing our self-identity patterns, and a host of other life events. I will refer to these fears as unhealthy and imaginary or established in our minds. They are blocking our personal growth and are the fears we need to examine and challenge.

The Divine Declaration

FEAR OF CHANGE

Imaginary fears are rooted in our minds. Their tentacles pervade our life and choke off growth and progress. We imagine negative situations, feed the worry, and sometimes obsess about the outcome. Think of the time you have dedicated to worrying or fretting over events that never occurred. These are the paralyzing what ifs. "If I lose my job, will I survive? If I change or stand up for my view, will I survive if others disagree? If I leave this unhealthy relationship, will I survive? If I move to another city, will I find a job and survive?" Or, simply, "If anything changes in my comfort zone, will I be able to cope?"

Some fears are directly related to survival of our physical bodies or belief systems. Some may be attached to physical safety, but other fears are without sound justification. Our fears include: animals (spiders, snakes, insects, mice), objects (computers, weapons), places (crowded, heights, dark, enclosed), events (failure, success, public speaking, crime, wars, job or relationship loss), disasters (weather, fire, car accident, death, financial), change (any change in life that expands our comfort zone), and people (rejection, authority, bullies, other cultures).

Remaining stuck in your fear immobilizes your growth and usually causes emotional pain. Your chances of becoming a healthy, self-actualized individual are diminished. Joy is practically non-existent and exciting ventures are not even in the realm of possibility. You are not able to trust anyone or anything when you live in fear.

When Jesus walked on water, his disciples wavered in their trust, feeling afraid and desperate for their safety. "And when the disciples saw him walking on the sea, they were troubled, saying, it is a spirit; and they cried out for fear."

Even with Jesus' reassurance, they struggled to trust.

Jesus said to them, "Be of good cheer; it is I; be not afraid."

Peter attempted to walk out to Jesus but was afraid and started sinking. "Lord, save me." he cried.

Jesus "stretched forth his hand and said unto him, 'O thou of little faith, wherefore didst thou doubt?'" [Matthew 14:26-31]

Peter's fear momentarily superseded his trust, and he was unable to walk on the water.

I have worked to overcome fear of success, failure, and ending relationships by releasing old patterns of self-identity and abandonment, but my fears played over in my mind: I really want to help people through my writing, but what if the book isn't all I want it to be? How much better will I relate if I interact in situations knowing that I am important, instead of feeling like a foster child? If I stand up for myself at work, will they kick me out like they would have in one of the foster homes? If I feel trapped in the status quo of the workaday world, will I have the courage to pursue my life purpose?

These specific fears prevented me from actually sitting down at the computer and writing, and living my dream. I soon realized that every time I sat at the computer and started typing, the information poured from my soul. I was in the "now" moment while writing, excited and feeling the divine connection as I typed the pages. Somehow I knew writing and helping others was my dream and I had to sit down and write through the fear. At times, it flowed, while other times I found excuses to delay the writing. However, I kept pushing on until I wrote a little more each time, exhilarated after completing a page, a chapter, or some really interesting research.

FEAR AND TERRORISM

We are now experiencing fear of terrorism worldwide. The September 11 attack on America challenged our sense of security. Life now includes speculation about the next attack and living with an elevated threat level. We are warned to be diligent and keep a watchful eye for terrorists. While the attack on the World Trade Center was a frightful and painful event for us all, we must live, work, play, and love. We cannot spend every moment in worry and fear of another attack. The media and our country's leaders tell us, "Go out and enjoy life. Fly and attend events, but make sure to keep a watchful eye."

If the other passengers who were on the flights with the terrorists on that dreadful day had obsessed and watched diligently, would they have noticed the box cutters? Probably not. We certainly need to be aware of the people around us, but we must live without paralyzing fear. Otherwise the terrorists, like our fears, have won, and we are perpetually paralyzed.

I discussed my fears with my brother. His light-hearted response to my concerns about going downtown for an appointment soon after the attack still makes me smile. He said, "They can only kill you once, and they can't eat you."

How true. My fear had spiraled, but his comment brought some much needed relief and returned me to a place of power.

FEAR IN THE WORKPLACE

The workplace can provide a breeding ground for the expression of fear. If management operates from fear, staff will typically follow its lead. Using fear as a motivational tool destroys morale and prevents organizations from succeeding. This fear model leads to office politics, competitive squabbling, a negative environment, and eventually, a fight-or-flight attitude. Employees come and go through a revolving door.

During my years in the corporate world, I have witnessed many examples of fear. Two specific examples of a fearful corporate culture come to mind and are especially worth noting.

In one of my workplace experiences, I was dismayed with the limited integrity and fear-based techniques. When I accepted the position, I discovered the adverse conditions faced by prior employees in my position, and how management remained indifferent to the situation because they were afraid to rock the boat. There was dishonesty in the organization, and employees were fearful. Several employees bulldozed over others. The steam rolling directly affected the income and production of the other employees. One employee who had been negatively affected left the company after a verbal altercation.

When it was my turn to interact with this group, it was difficult to take a stand. Only after several encounters did my fear, emotional attachment, and disappointment give way to a sense of feeling my own personal power. I knew I must face the fear of rejection and again, take back my power. With trepidation I addressed each incident as it occurred. Through determination and a strong belief in universal abundance, I survived and actually created success in this unhealthy environment.

In another workplace experience, I observed rampant fear in a culture toxic to the employees. In this case, a few top management employees embezzled from the company as a means of getting what they wanted and perhaps to satisfy their subconscious resentment. The corporate culture was one of hostility and fear. Top and middle management enforced the rules with a heavy hand, and the employee turnover was high. Embezzlement, underhanded tactics, and mean spiritedness were the *soup du jour* most every day, at least for some of the upper management. One of the managers admitted he enjoyed pitting people against each other and watching them squirm. Strict rules and regulations and expected long work hours, combined with suppressing creativity by discounting ideas for improvement, contributed to the emotionally toxic atmosphere. Everyone functioned as a means to an end for the owners.

After I left this workplace, I could clearly see that I had been in a dysfunctional environment. This type of dictator management is not conducive to empowerment and creativity. Management thought by keeping people in fear and treating them as insignificant, it had the power, when in fact, most of the employees were disgruntled, resentful, and happy to move on.

FEAR IN RELATIONSHIPS

Have you ever ended an unhealthy relationship? We are often afraid of rejection and failure. People may remain in unhealthy relationships because they fear physical harm, they feel overly responsible, or they have low self-esteem and are operating in a co-dependent situation. Others choose financial security over happiness and feel uneasy about living alone.

My foster mother, the one with whom I have been since age sixteen, pressed through her fear of financial insecurity when she left a marriage of twenty-one years and decided to strike out on her own without a safety net. At the time, her job of ten years provided her with a comfortable living, but she had no one on whom to rely if she encountered financial difficulty. Since ending that relationship, she has purchased two homes and is now retired with an adequate income. Facing her fear step-by-step allowed her a unique freedom and opportunity for spiritual and personal growth, which she draws upon daily.

CONQUERING FEAR

In Susan Jeffers' book, *Feel the Fear and Do it Anyway*, she carefully takes her reader through the steps of working through fear. She tells us to remember the phrase, "I can handle anything."

What a powerful statement! You may want to sit with this statement a moment and allow it to sink in. Recall it whenever you feel overwhelmed to strengthen your resolve.

We build confidence and grow through confronting our fears. We expand our comfort zones and our lives as we conquer our fears. Each time I sit and write another page, my fear lessens. Each time I stand up for myself in a difficult situation, I have more courage than before. Each time I experience success, I am able to absorb the successful feeling a little more. As for failure, is there really any

The Divine Declaration

failure, or are there simply lessons we use to determine what we do not desire in our lives? I choose to believe we are learning lessons and there really is no failure *per se*, because in review of the events in my life I thought were failures at the time, such as getting out of an unhealthy marriage or changing jobs, I find now that I was learning what did not work in my life through those experiences. However, it would be more peaceful to learn through "ease and grace," as my friend often says.

As we examine fear, we might consider Roosevelt's words, "The only thing we have to fear is fear itself."

Or Emerson's, "Fear defeats more people than any other one thing in the world."

Fear thou not, for I am with thee...

There are various schools of thought on how to overcome fear. Some experts recommend behavioral changes. In other words, when you do what you fear, the fear will dissipate as you face it and engage in the process. You talk about it, unearth the root, and uproot the fear in your mind through cognitive therapy.

The most effective process I have found is to awaken to your spiritual power. Through this awakening, you will find a greater sense of safety. You will awaken to the understanding that the eternal you, your Divine Self, is unharmed by physical or verbal attacks. Your Divine Self is where your power lies and where fear does not live.

I have used a combination of these processes and found them to be effective. However, it is through the spiritual awakening of my Divine Inner Power that has overwhelmingly created the lasting results.

God has not given us the spirit of fear, but of love...

Thru belief in the Word

I can do all things thru Christ which strengthens me...

Resistance to Your Divine Inner Power

SELF-ESTEEM

Self-esteem plays a critical role in our lives. It is the foundation of our self-value. Nathaniel Branden, psychotherapist, author, and pioneer in the field of self-esteem, argues that "Of all the judgments that we pass in life, none is as important as the one we pass on ourselves, for that judgment touches the very center of our existence."

How an individual views himself or herself affects the fabric of relationships, academic and career decisions, success, health, and a general attitude about life. According to Branden,

> *The nature of his self-evaluation has profound effects on a man's thinking processes, emotions, desires, values, and goals. It is the single most significant key to his behavior. To understand a man psychologically, one must understand the nature and degree of his self-esteem, and the standards by which he judges himself.*

If someone lacks self-esteem, he or she may be forced to fake self-worth and live in a mask. This person uses the ego as a prop, and may be overly arrogant, insensitive to others, abrasive, controlling and intimidating, bullying, cold, aloof, untrustworthy, excessively ambitious and competitive, or adept at playing emotional politics. Low self-esteem may also be the root cause of low performance, some poverty, crime, and drug addiction.

Healthy or unhealthy self-esteem originates in childhood. Parental and authoritative figures mirror the child's value because the child looks to them with awe and vulnerability. While this mirroring may not wholly constitute the individual's self-esteem, it is significant in the child's development. When we are acknowledged and praised for a job well done, our self-esteem increases. Conversely, if we are constantly criticized, lack support from our parents or the adults in our life whom we admire, and feel that we "don't measure up," our self-esteem lags and we question our worthiness. This feeling of not being good enough is also promoted through excessive praise that does not meet the reality of the situation.

We are all worthy and divine. If we did not receive the support needed when we were young, we can work later in life to build our self-esteem and nourish our connection with our Divine Inner Power. [Thru the Holy Spirit]

Organizations, systems, and environments may also discourage a healthy self-view. One example is the overpowering boss who negates employees through consistent criticism, or a manager who makes a habit of disempowering employees by <u>dismissing</u> their ideas and <u>suppressing</u> individual and professional development. Another example of this organizational suppression is revealed through the fear featured in some teachings that instill the message "you're not worthwhile and you're lucky that God loves you," either through subtle conditioning or verbal admonition. This type of teaching is disjointed and disconnected from a God of love, and leads to a convoluted and blocked sense of *Self*.

<u>Unhealthy</u> parental relationships, other authoritative adult relationships, and fear-based organizational values are not the only attacks on self-esteem. The emotional damage may also be perpetuated through an unhealthy romantic relationship. <u>Any relationship that is unsupportive</u> and laden with childhood emotional issues is a dagger in the heart of our self-esteem. A person involved in a damaging relationship may feel actual physical pain in the chest and

solar-plexus. The emotional roller coaster in an unhealthy relationship may result from overt or covert abuse. Abuse to the psyche may stem from physical abuse, emotional abuse, or both. Physical abuse delivers a visible wound to the body and a damaging blow to the emotional body and spirit. Emotional abuse is a covert wound to the emotional body and spirit. These covert wounds may not produce immediate devastation as the physical abuse does, but over time they insidiously, with venomous poison, erode and destroy self-esteem.

At age two, my father passed away and my mother allowed us to be placed in foster care. My self-esteem suffered a severe blow that I have worked through as an adult to heal. The family with whom I was initially placed provided a loving, stable, and supportive environment for five years. My next foster home was marked by parental indifference that lasted for another eight years. During this difficult period, my foster sister and her family from my first home contributed a strong, positive intervention that held me steady. My natural older brothers and sisters were also part of my support system. Finally, I moved in with my final foster parents at age sixteen. The wounds to my self-esteem started very early and weren't quite healed during my formative years.

My wounded self-esteem led me into an ill-advised marriage in which I thought I could save my partner. We shared a common bond: we were both gymnasts. He was not living up to his potential, and I thought on some level that I could help him. This emotional task was, of course, a disaster. I had attracted someone with an unhealthy self-esteem, similar to the level of my own self-esteem at that time.

The Divine Declaration

I was a frightened girl with a vision to save someone, anyone, and maybe I would be saved in the process.

My ex-husband, without malice, stepped in emotionally where my biological parents left off. There was never any physical abuse, but the emotional roller coaster was an endurance test, much like my foster home with the indifferent parent.

Eventually, I left the marriage without knowing what direction to take. I knew for sure this was not a happy relationship and I wanted a new life. The stress of the marriage was another blow to my sense of *Self*. Later in counseling, as I viewed the relationship under the microscope of self-examination, I recognized the emotional abandonment similarity between my marital relationship and my biological mother allowing me to be placed in foster care. Like my biological mother, my ex-husband could not emotionally connect with me.

During the separation from my ex-husband, I began sessions with a pastoral counselor. The first question I posed to him was, "Should I divorce my husband?"

His direct and most appropriate response surprised me. "Let's not focus on whether or not you should divorce your husband," he replied. "Instead, let's talk about why you were attracted to him in the first place."

The counseling sessions exposed the connection of my present situation to the past and much more. The counselor helped me understand my motivations based on past experiences. Step-by-step he helped me leave my unhealthy marriage and reclaim my sense of *Self*.

To overcome low self-esteem, you must be honest with yourself regarding how you really feel about who you are. Do you view yourself as worthwhile and deserving, and does your outer life reflect this view? Are you living in peace, love, health, and abundance? Was your support system as a child critical or supportive? What kind of relationships are in your life — supportive or destructive? Do they bring you energy or sap your energy? Are you happy with your personal achievements? Are you living in your divine, right livelihood? Do you feel enthusiasm and divine energy in your life?

If you can answer these questions in the positive, you are in a great position to connect with your Divine Inner Power and elevate your life another step. If there are areas in which you need a helping hand in order to boost your self-esteem, more help is on the way.

HIERARCHY OF NEEDS

Abraham Maslow's Hierarchy of Needs illustrates the process leading to self-esteem and eventually transcendence. Maslow's research indicates the need to satisfy each level of development prior to moving up to the next one. Basic needs such as food and water, environmental safety, and a loving environment where you can flourish are the primary components of the foundation necessary to ascend to the desire to learn new ideas and enjoy cultural and artistic expression. For instance, if you were without food, water, and shelter, these needs would likely override the urge to attend a museum exhibit.

There are also times when we vacillate between the levels. Perhaps one day you may feel secure in your job, and the next day you may question that security. Meeting these needs at each level fosters progression to understanding the *Self,* aspiring to live up to one's potential, and upward to self-transcendence. Helping others find fulfillment in their lives and realize their potential is a rewarding aspect of self-transcendence.

The Hierarchy of Needs pyramid is organized as follows:

1. Physiological Needs – These are basic needs that affect physical well-being (food, water, vitamins and minerals, sleep, exercise, and pain avoidance).

2. Safety/Security Needs – Once the physiological needs are met, the second level is addressed. Shelter, job security, safe environments for work and home life, and retirement planning are part of the safety/security issues.

3. Belongingness and Love Needs – When we are comfortable that our physical needs and our safety/security needs are being met, we step up to the need of love and belonging. At this level we seek connection with our family, friends, lovers, children or pets, memberships in organizations, or community involvement.

4. Esteem Needs – Next, we begin to need self-esteem. We seek respect from others, recognition, attention, fame, and fortune on a lower level. On the higher level of self-esteem, we seek self-respect, independence, confidence, and our own competent level.

5. Self-Actualization – At this level, we are able to discern between what is genuine and what is fake. We become better problem solvers and enjoy our solitude and deep personal relationships with a few friends and family members rather than shallow relationships with numerous people. We

become mavericks or non-conformists, not accepting social pressure to fit in. A sense of humor without hostility is developed at this level. We also prefer being ourselves as opposed to pretending we are something else in order to gain acceptance. This level includes respect for others and strong ethics accompanied by spirituality, but rarely with a narrow dogma.

6. Self-Transcendence – After self-actualization, we move to the level of self-transcendence, where we seek to help others live up to their potential.

Maslow's Hierarchy of Needs leads us to understand the ascending process of self-actualization and transcendence. By understanding this process, we are equipped to work on attaining each successive stage in the process.

The following diagram illustrates Maslow's Hierarchy of Needs.

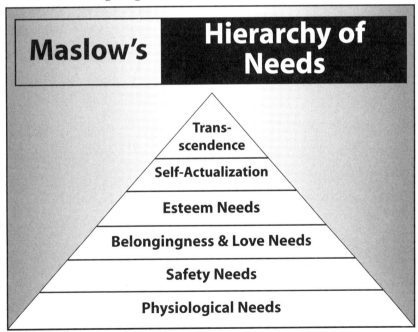

The Divine Declaration

A healthy self-esteem leads to greater objectivity as we meet life's challenges. When we enjoy a deep sense of our value, if someone slights us or our feelings are hurt, we simply recognize, feel, release the pain, and move on. A healthy self-esteem supports the pursuit of our dreams and goals. We do not obsess over every challenging event, and find we are able to move forward with enthusiasm and dedication. We know at a deep level we will master the challenge.

With a healthy sense of *Self* and an awareness of our connection with the divine nature of God, we value ourselves and our relationships with others. We do not require the "whip" of controlling belief systems to live a worthwhile, loving life, and to contribute in a positive way to our universe. When we are connected to our Divine Inner Power, the love and caring nature of our real *Self* is alive and well. This is the nature of Jesus, Gandhi, Martin Luther King, the Dalai Lama, and Mother Teresa. I have also witnessed this *Self* alive in people I have encountered in my daily life who feel their connection to a loving God and who are able to extend themselves to others through their actions and not just their words. They are not self-absorbed, hurtful, or disinterested. They are giving and loving by nature. Healthy self-esteem does not equate to self-absorption or ego-based selfishness, but reveals itself through true love and self-acceptance.

In other words, "You can tell how a man feels about himself by how he treats his fellow man."

People who feel good about themselves care about others. Conversely, people with low self-esteem or who are out of touch with their own Divine Inner Power may be hurtful to others. We project onto others how we feel about ourselves. When we feel we have value, we seek to have a positive impact in the world. I believe if everyone had self-esteem and lived in connection with his or her divine power, there would be more harmony and compassion and less hatred and wars.

OLD NEGATIVE PROGRAMMING

Old negative programming may also block our divine power connection. The programming we receive at a young age establishes a baseline for our automatic belief system. If we are abandoned at an early age or if our parents are emotionally unavailable to us, we perceive ourselves as unlovable. As children, we process emotionally, not rationally, and therefore, we feel the pain. Because we are the center of our universe at an early age, this distance from our parents, whether emotionally or physically, is absorbed as, "There must be something wrong with me. My parents, who are all-knowing in my world, do not love me."

This negative programming is devastating for a child. When a belief system is set at an early age and then reinforced throughout childhood, it requires personal growth work as an adult to change the beliefs and reconnect with our divinity.

The negative program scripts might include the following:

> Negative beliefs about yourself such as, "If my parents couldn't love me, who will?"

> Negative comments about you from your family or peers that you remember and hold on to

> Negative self-images relating to your physical appearance

> Anger and resentment toward people who may have knowingly or unknowingly hurt you
> Responsibility for others
> Jealousy
> Feelings of inferiority
> A sense of unworthiness, abandonment, or rejection
> Anxiety around what others think of you
> Being overly submissive or agreeable
> Playing a role such as "damsel in distress," "clown," or "controller"

Playing these scripts in your mind contributes to lack of self-esteem and hinders your ability to connect with and utilize your divine power. Your mind may be so filled with this negative programming, there is no room left to relax and connect.

As I mentioned earlier, when I was two, my father passed away and my mother released my five siblings and me into foster care. Today, forty years later, I continue peering through the tattered remains of this veil of abandonment, and with each day, month, and year I lift the veil higher and see the light of my inner *Self*. It is through inner work, and the caring, compassionate help from others that I have been able to move through the emotional issues surrounding my childhood, and peel away the layers of pain. I have read, written, meditated, prayed, cried, laughed, and talked through the obstacles that paralyzed my sense of *Self*.

Hope exists for you, too, to regain your sense of *Self* if you have negative childhood programming. It can be very painful if your parents were absent (emotionally or physically), or if they were bogged down in their own issues and projected their frustrations and anger onto you, leaving you feeling unimportant or mistreated. However, you can move through the pain and into your power.

While most childhood experiences are not like the Cleavers of the television show *Leave it to Beaver* (even those were questionable — Mrs. Cleaver dressed for the dinner table as if she were going out somewhere for the evening. Some children may have found this a little intimidating on a daily basis), some were quite difficult to survive. Enduring alcoholic parents and physical abuse or tolerating emotional and mental abuse in quiet desperation results in visible or hidden wounds. Both leave deep, hidden scars.

Negative programming also occurs through peer relationships. Enduring bullying in school is emotionally damaging. A bullied child may feel helpless and useless. Not being accepted by our peers is another severe blow to self-esteem.

I know someone who endured severe bullying in middle and high school. His life today is much less than it could be. He is smart, funny, and talented, but the emotional damage, from the bullying he survived, has left an indelible scar on his view of his personal value. He internalized their taunting.

Although I have told him what the bullies did to him was a reflection of their sense of *Self*, not his, this is difficult for him to believe. After all, he has played those tapes for a lifetime.

Negative programming experienced during childhood often affects us subconsciously until we discover the patterns and stop the madness. We may seek relationships that replicate our relationship with the parent with whom we have emotional issues. For instance,

The Divine Declaration

a woman whose father was emotionally or physically absent in childhood may pursue romantic relationships with men who are also emotionally unavailable. They may be commitment-phobic or have other emotional issues. She may be attracted to men who are charmers and remain emotionally detached by dating several women. These men represent her absent father. Subconsciously, this emotional chase is familiar. Then one day she tires of the chase and says, "No more." At this point, she may decide to reconnect with her power and stop chasing an elusive, hypothetical individual.

Another example of this cycle is men choosing romantic relationships with women who remind them of their mothers. The woman may be distant and aloof, playing the waiting game to catch her man. Others may be demanding. As she dictates, he becomes the child, and she, the mother figure. Quite common is the man seeking control of the damsel in distress. The damsel needs something from him. He gives and controls her in exchange for her needing him financially or emotionally. At first, and sometimes throughout the relationship, she allows him to take charge and appear in control, meanwhile the dance of "one upmanship" plays out. For example, she may be emotionally distressed, or need a place to live or someone to lean on. She needs him to take care of her, and he is willing to fill the bill in order to gain control. These mental dances require inner work and acceptance to end the perpetual, unfulfilling cycle and fully embrace an authentic, loving relationship.

We may also exhibit childhood programming in other arenas of our lives. Our work environment yields fertile ground for working through our issues. I once worked in a dishonest and unhealthy work environment. Due to fear of conflict, management looked the other way; thereby, endorsed the dishonesty. The dishonesty directly affected me, and when I brought it to light, the manager was noticeably displeased. He simply didn't want to be involved.

I was disappointed, but soon recognized I was projecting my "foster child" identity onto the situation. In my emotional construct, the owner was the foster parent, and the manager and other employees were the chosen ones he favored. This experience forced me to face my programming. I learned to stand up for myself and speak out with a voice I had suppressed for years. The confrontation was uncomfortable, and I feared that I would be thrown out, just as I had felt in one of the foster homes where I thought I would be thrown out if I verbalized an opinion. The lesson was that it was more important for me to stand up for myself than to stay in the fold.

The programming we receive as children has a tremendous impact on how we relate to ourselves and others as adults. If we received negative programming, we must work to overcome the fears generated from this experience. Even with this obstacle, we can move forward, connect with our Divine Inner Power, ascend the Hierarchy of Needs, and stand tall. On this journey we learn who we are and to love ourselves wholly.

The Divine Declaration II — Releasing Resistance to My Divinity and Divine Power

When in the course of my life, I find repression, unhappiness, ill-health, a chaotic state of mind, and a general sense of hopelessness, it is essential that I release any old programming, ties to the past, current situations, or people who do not support my happiness, my ability to pursue my dreams, my general well-being, and my spiritual, emotional, and mental growth. I now assume my connection to God, the Divine Source, and recognize the power residing inside of me. I was created by the Divine Source; therefore, it must hold true that I am connected to this divinity and have access to a greater power. It is inside of me. It is my divine inheritance. I choose a new path of freedom from the albatross of unworthiness today. The weight is gone. A new world awaits me. And, so it is.

Thank you, Universe. Thank you, God.

I now accept as true and hold these truths to be evident: I choose my world today. I will be courageous and deal with my fears directly. I know in my heart that the Divine Source wants my best; therefore, there is only hope. The fear that is paralyzing my life and delaying my dreams is an imaginary obstacle in my life, something that I can remove by changing my view of the fear. I choose to face the fear, do whatever it takes to let go of it, and take back my power. My self-esteem is critical to my success and happiness. It is my gauge of how I treat myself. I am worthy, and, regardless of past circumstances, I have great value. I love myself more and more each day. I see the little child in me, and I nurture that child with love, respect, and emotional support. I forgive myself for past mistakes and forgive others who may have hurt me intentionally or unintentionally. It is for my own sake that I release this old tattered pain of the past. I determine my own worth based on my own value system. I know that I am a child of God, and the child part of me that was hurt is also a child of God. I live acknowledging my divine inheritance. I know that I have worth. I move forward in life, decide the life I want, and take the steps to manifest my dreams. My life choices now belong to me. There is no one to blame. I am strong. I am powerful. I am divine. It is through this divine connection that I fly from the nest to live my dreams. There is nothing to fear. I am worthy and powerful, and the past is healed.

The future is bright for me. My present thoughts are creating my life from this day forward. My highest good is manifesting in greater ways than I ever imagined.

This is my Divine Declaration.

Section Two

Examine the Power of Your Thoughts

Chapter Three

How Your Thoughts Affect Your Life

The Divine Declaration

"Life externalizes at the level of our thought."
— Ernest Holmes

How Your Thoughts Affect Your Life

What you are thinking now is creating your life. Stop for a moment and identify your thoughts. Are they positive or negative? When you recall your daily thoughts, do you focus mostly on what is wrong in your life rather than creating the life you want? You build your life by the blueprint and foundation of your thoughts. How would you like your life to look? Would you like a life built firmly on a foundation of happiness, health, abundance, love, and peace? A constructed building reflects the blueprint; your world reflects your belief system.

It's time to start contemplating and developing your life's desires. Leave misery and unhappiness behind you. Thoughts of unworthiness have no place with you now. Your new line of thinking is moving toward alignment with the life you wish to create. Positive thinking is a cornerstone for creating the life you want to live. Like attracts like: positive attracts positive, negative attracts negative.

HOW THOUGHTS CREATE

We are constantly thinking, and these thoughts are creating our life experience. Thought is the seed planted in the soil of our subconscious mind. With enough nurturing, the seed grows into the form of our lives. If we plant thoughts of great things happening, we will follow this line of growth. If we focus on how terrible things are and live in the "I can't" mode, that will be the direction of growth our life will follow.

Life is your garden. Planting a specific seed will grow a specific plant. An acorn will grow an oak, and a wildflower seed will produce a beautiful wildflower. Therefore, we must know what we want to plant and grow in our lives. Plant the seed in your mind and nurture its growth. Without a plan or direction for your life, you may harvest what someone else planted and left behind or whatever seeds blow on the wind.

Your thoughts have their own energy, and energy has its own vibration. Your energy has your vibratory signature, and your thoughts vibrate at a positive or negative rate. This concept relates to the science of basic energy. Some examples of energy are: kinetic energy — the energy of motion, and potential energy — stored energy that becomes kinetic at the point of conversion to movement, mechanical energy, electrical energy, atomic energy, thermal energy, magnetic energy, and chemical energy.

All matter consists of atoms containing a nucleus of protons and neutrons. Electrons orbit the protons and neutrons on energetic levels that stabilize the atom. Higher electron orbits occur through elevated energy, and the electrons release energy as they downgrade to a lower orbit. If atoms are in alignment, they move forward in a common direction, such as a magnet that attracts through this "common goal" or molecular process.

How Your Thoughts Affect Your Life

Your thoughts, energy, and vibrations equally attract at a positive or negative level. When you are in joy, feeling gracious and alive, you attract more of that positive energy through your own vibrations. If your thought vibrations sink to a lower level of despair or fear, you release your positive energy. You will notice your energy drop from enthusiasm and zest to lethargy and negativity. This lower vibratory level attracts more of the same low energy.

Energetic vibration and the Law of Attraction are powerful forces interacting with our thoughts and creating our worlds. Where our focus is or whatever the level of our thoughts, positive or negative, we are, knowingly or unknowingly, creating more of this energy in our lives. Focusing your thoughts on what you want to create forms a space of "creation and knowing," a place of stabilized energy working to create and manifest your life dreams. Reaching a place of "knowing that you know that you know" is a process you can build on day-by-day. Your belief strengthens as you work in harmony with your thought process. Jesus acknowledged this law of "thoughts create" in Mark 11:23 —

> *Whosoever shall say unto this mountain, Be thou removed, and be thou cast into the sea; and shall not doubt in his heart, but shall believe that those things which he saith shall come to pass; he shall have whatsoever he saith.*

Ernest Holmes, in *The Science of Mind*, again explains this law —

> *We must say that all thought is creative, according to nature, impulse, emotion or conviction behind the thought. Thought creates a mold in the Subjective, in which the idea is accepted and poured, and sets power in motion in accordance with the thought. Ignorance*

of this excuses no one from its effects, for we are dealing with Law and not with whimsical fancy.

Following your intuition also reinforces this "knowing" process. Each time you follow your intuition and find your hunch confirmed, it reinforces your faith in your intuition and "knowing that you know that you know."

Our subconscious or subjective mind connects to this thought energy. Our subconscious is the point of contact with the universal ONE power. We drink from the well of our subconscious mind. The thoughts we pour into it are from the stream of our conscious thoughts and belief patterns. This is our creative medium, and we utilize it even if we do not realize it. When we realize this connection, we can access this infinite fountain flowing with transformative power.

We project our physical existence from our thoughts and belief system. If we subconsciously send out patterns of fear and failure, we will experience this in our life. Reprogram your subconscious mind through your conscious thoughts and you will transform your life. Changing our thought patterns and belief system transforms a fearful or empty existence into a life filled with opportunities and choices, into the life we desire.

The conscious mind is the filter and gateway to the subconscious. During the course of our lifetime, our overpowering thought pattern or prominent belief system seeps through to the subconscious mind or creative medium. The subconscious accepts our programs. It does not distinguish between what is real among your creative imagination, visualizations, and deep-seated beliefs. It works with you to create your reality based on the information (your thoughts, imagination, and continuous belief patterns) you are feeding it.

You can reformat this filtered information any time you choose, but you must also choose to examine what is flowing through the filter that affects your life. Is your filter clogged with negativity, or are you cleaning it regularly with positive information and allowing new life to flow through? Releasing old patterns that aren't creating what you want in life and transitioning into patterns aligned with your Divine Inner Power will allow you to take flight to a new life. You will find it no longer necessary to drag around the albatross of negative energy. Like an eagle perched high upon a ledge, you are at the threshold of power and freedom.

NOURISHING YOUR THOUGHTS

Once we decide what we would like to manifest in our lives, we either stunt our growth through negativity or nurture it with positive nourishment. Your life can be stunted by fear, frustration, or hopelessness, or you can flourish in an environment illuminated by the sunlight of positive thinking, enthusiasm, anticipation of great things in life, and an affirmative, prayerful way of living.

If our thoughts live in the barren soil of negative energy, we create and attract at that level. Notice when you dislike someone, you develop an attitude about that person. You may be impatient or have a tone of irritation. As a result, they receive your negative energy and many times reflect it by responding with abruptness or in an abrasive tone.

Other examples of negative thinking are fear, anger, and

unhappiness. Notice how your world reflects your dominant thought pattern. Your energy or vibration is intermingling with the energetic vibration around you, expanding or attracting more of that energy. You may not recognize this concept and wonder, "Why is this thing happening to me?" However, if you reflect on your thoughts before a negative encounter, you may discover a negative thought pattern. The pattern may have been one of fear, anger, depression, frustration, or irritability.

To change these thoughts and change your life, let's look at how to improve a negative outlook and to step forward to a positive life. First, you must honestly examine your thought patterns to determine what you frequently feed into your subconscious mind. Is it fear, depression, or living in a hang dog, deadpan frame of mind, or are you enthusiastic and excited about what could happen in your life, appreciating the wonderful things you have already accomplished? These are two very different ways of creating or manifesting life. Henry Ford said, "If you think you can or you think you can't, you will always be right."

I remember a time in my professional life when Henry Ford's words resonated. I accepted an advertising sales position with a magazine after one person resigned to pursue another career, and the next person in the position was relieved because she was having difficulty rebuilding the sales territory. The position was challenging. The territory was barren and hadn't been profitable for a couple of years. I knew rebuilding the territory would be like carving a creation from stone, but I decided to stick it out. To focus interest on my territory and to spur sales, I asked that it be more frequently highlighted in the magazine's editorial calendar. I also built a new database of contacts and proceeded to sell, sell, sell. I mailed information to every name I could enter into the database. Even if they didn't buy advertising right away, at least they would know who we were. Through my strong belief in universal abundance coupled with hard work, I doubled the sales in the territory. I thought I could, and I did.

At the other end of the spectrum of how our thoughts create, someone once told me not to have expectations, "Then you will not be disappointed." That philosophy is correct. Not expecting anything great to come your way is sure to manifest that condition. If you expect nothing, you get nothing, a process that leads to apathy rather than disappointment. However, apathy is a bland way to exist.

To shift your thoughts from negative to positive, consciously engage in a process that reverses the negativity preventing you from living your dreams. As soon as you realize you're in a negative holding pattern, change your flight plan. The controls are in your hands. God and the universe are the wind beneath your wings. You have control of the craft; you decide if you crash or soar.

CHANGE YOUR THOUGHTS

Changing your thought process may be challenging at first, but like riding a bicycle or learning to walk, it will eventually become second nature. Sit quietly for a moment and feel your mind racing. Then check in with your body and feel the tension connected to the thoughts of the day. Perhaps your thoughts are of work, traffic jams, or the news you heard on television or radio. These negative thoughts racing through your mind contribute to muscle tension, high blood pressure, and various other physical ailments. Negative energy created from negative thinking is permeating the cells of your body and surrounding your physical *Self*. This energy is interacting with the energy around you and intermingling to create your life. When you're thinking heavy, negative thoughts, your energy is constricted, making it difficult to attract or release. Your energy is locked in position, frozen. To unfreeze your position and free your energy to expand, attract your desires, and release the pain, change your thought pattern.

Living in a negative pattern or a fight-or-flight mode is taxing on your body. Subconsciously, I decided early in life to hold on to people and things if at all possible. The thought of losing another person in my life or the possibility of my life spiraling out of control kept me in a state of holding on. My body paid a high price for the years of experiencing a child's fear of rejection and the internal demand to perform, to "be as good as." I tightly held on to the old thought process I needed as a child to survive. This emotional construct created negative energy in my physical body. It was stored in the parts of my body mirroring these desperate thoughts. I experienced chronic neck pain. My shoulder and neck muscles were so tense they wouldn't relax.

The neck, where the throat chakra resides, represents expression. Interestingly, when I spent several weeks very focused on writing this book, I did not experience any neck pain.

My holding is also represented by Irritable Bowel Syndrome (IBS) and reflects my mentally and emotionally holding on to old things I no longer need. I had built a long-term pattern of holding on to old

How Your Thoughts Affect Your Life

clothing, unnecessary papers, and unhealthy relationships. I simply did not want to let things go. After working diligently on this issue, I'm less anxious when releasing unhealthy relationships and unnecessary or worn-out items. I find it easier to release the old and allow space for the new.

When you revise your thought pattern, your energetic composition changes. Because of this change, you stand more erect with your head held a little higher; you walk a little lighter.

To demonstrate this change, switch your thoughts for a few moments and feel the difference in your body and your energy. Think of a meadow or a beautiful landscape. Feel it completely. Now think of something that prompts a smile (I think of my puppies and an automatic smile appears). Recall a pleasant memory from your childhood. It may spark another smile. Now, allow your thoughts to drift to your lover or anyone you dearly love and who is supportive of you. Then follow your thoughts through to how your body feels now.

I keep photos of my puppies, on my desk at work, to help me stay centered and to spark a smile if I am having a tough day. You might consider this option for your work environment or any place you need a reminder of the wonderful things in your life. When you smile, you feel a change in energy. Surround your space with items that bring a smile, and with elements of happiness that will help you during stressful times. Read an uplifting book, quote, or anecdote to brighten a dark mood. I have the quote by Marianne Williamson, referenced earlier in Chapter One, on the bulletin board in my office. These are life icons that promote positive thinking.

Positive thinking, like keeping physically fit, is not something you practice once and expect continued results. It is something you must practice frequently if you want your life to stay in shape. We do not exercise one time and expect our bodies to stay fit. A fit mental, spiritual, and emotional state also requires commitment and exercise. We cannot just believe positive thinking works and do nothing about it. We must exercise positive thinking.

Just as a computer is hampered by viruses, we are hampered by low-level vibrations and negative energy. As we work on our spiritual development and exercise our positive thinking, eventually, or in an instant if we choose, we can use the firewall of spirituality to buffer negative vibrations.

Knowing that God or Divine Source is the only law and that we are connected to this divinity is extremely powerful. When we reach this level of consciousness and know that Infinite Divinity is the law that runs the universe, we can release any claims and battles of unhappiness or poverty consciousness. There is no opposition, nothing to battle. There is one law and it is good, loving, supportive, and always within reach of your awakening.

We can connect to this Divine Inner Power whenever we choose. Meditation is an effective way to access this level of awareness (see Chapter Five for process examples). If we slow the thoughts racing through the highways of our mind, we open our channels to enlightenment and allow space for God or the Divine Source to speak to us in these quiet moments.

Meditation also helps us to open to divine awareness during our struggle in illusory battles with others who may be stuck in the physical mire and who encroach on our very existence. We might ask,

How Your Thoughts Affect Your Life

"How dare they throw stones in the calm waters of our life?" When we own our divinity and our inner power, the stones thrown our way are deflected. The meteor shower of negative energy that threatens us ceases, and our energy remains calm and peaceful.

In Baird Spalding's *Life and Teaching of the Masters of the Far East*, the spiritual masters with whom he traveled encountered a group of bandits approaching them. A master sent love from his calm, still center to this dangerous group of bandits and the bandits' negative energy couldn't penetrate the wall of love and light. Their own negative energy turned upon them. The master never raised a weapon.

Another process to develop a healthy state of spiritual, mental, and emotional health and to revise our thought pattern is through the use of affirmations and techniques you will find in Chapter Five. These techniques are valuable tools for confirming our truth and counteracting the negative hypnotism of others. We must begin to understand that other people are projecting what is inside of them, not who we are. Terry Cole Whittaker addresses this concept in her book, *What You Think of Me Is None of My Business*. When someone is treating you in a way that is less than loving, remember the negative verbal attacks or acts of superiority indicate something out of alignment inside of that individual, not the truth of who they are or the truth of who you are.

"When someone diminishes another person, he also diminishes himself. You cannot sink your shipmates without also sinking yourself" are quotes of real wisdom. We are all in the same boat connected by the ONE energy. These are excellent gauges to use when interacting with others. As you connect to your own Divine

The Divine Declaration

Inner Power, you recognize the fear and unhappiness within the individual who treats others with disregard and indifference, and you do not allow it to negatively affect you.

When you observe someone mistreating an animal, do you think the animal must somehow be at fault or inferior to the person? Of course not. The animal is a divine part of the Creator and love in physical form. The person mistreating the animal is totally out of touch with his or her divinity and is projecting this disconnection onto the animal. The animal is divine. Whether or not the person recognizes this divinity is within each individual.

Do we think of this concept when remembering mistreatment as a child? Not usually. We feel we must have in some way been at fault and the parental or authoritative figures were all-knowing. We feel, on a subconscious level, if they abandoned or mistreated us, we must have deserved the mistreatment or created it on some level. To clarify this concept, think of a great work of art. If someone lacks appreciation for the Mona Lisa, does this devalue the painting? Absolutely not. My foster mother once said to me when I was distraught that someone had hurt my feelings, "Look at what they did to Jesus. He was caring, compassionate, and spiritually evolved. They nailed him to a cross. And you expect everyone to like you?"

It is simply not realistic to assume that everyone will like you. It really doesn't matter if everyone likes you. What is important is if you like you.

You will encounter people with emotional baggage and something about you triggers their issues. They will begin projecting these issues onto you. When you are faced with someone's programming, remember it is his or her programming, and you do not have to agree to it or absorb it.

You can choose your thoughts and beliefs that define who you are. Use the process in this book to undo and reprogram your divine data. Reconnect your thoughts to your divinity. This connection is an essential part of taking back your power. There is a time of revelation and a deep level of knowing your connection to your Divine Inner Power. You will "know that you know that you know." This knowing brings with it peace, understanding, and steadfastness. You reach a place of centeredness, and as you engage in your spiritual development, you find it is indeed a process. Revelations may happen sporadically and quickly, or it may take some time to assimilate new concepts. Be patient with yourself, and know that you are elevating your height of understanding and personal power.

A few years ago I was discussing enlightenment with John Harricharan, a spiritual lecturer and author of several books. I asked him how he had gained so much wisdom and insight. He answered wisely, "It was an evolution, not a revolution."

Like a flower, the spiritual evolution of your life will blossom as you accept the positive light of connecting with your Divine Inner Power.

You may use the Divine Declaration at the end of this chapter to help you with the process of changing your thoughts and reaching the place of "knowing that you know that you know."

The Divine Declaration III – My Thoughts are Creating My Life

When in the course of my life, I find repression, unhappiness, ill health, a chaotic state of mind, and a general sense of hopelessness, it is essential that I release any old programming, ties to the past, current situations, or people who are not supportive of my happiness, my ability to pursue my dreams, my general well-being, and my spiritual, emotional, and mental growth. I now assume my connection to God, the Divine Source, and recognize the power residing inside of me. I was created by the Divine Source; therefore, it must hold true that I am connected to this divinity and have access to a greater power. It is inside of me. It is my divine inheritance. I choose a new path of freedom from the albatross of unworthiness today. The weight is gone. A new world awaits me. And, so it is.

Thank you, Universe. Thank you, God.

How Your Thoughts Affect Your Life

I now accept as true and hold these truths to be evident: I live in the divine light because I am a part of God or All That Is. I am in divine guidance each and every day. Everything I do and say is divinely guided. My thoughts are creating my experience. I believe the truth of my divine connection to God, and universal power is the real me. Therefore, I am always connected to my divinity, love, and life expression. I can believe in my good and I do. My highest good is always available. I allow it into my experience now. When I tune into my divine power, I create the life I want to live. I create the form for my life through my conscious thoughts, fill it with the substance through my feelings of faith and enthusiasm, and experience my highest good in the physical realm. I live in universal abundance, health, happiness, peace, and love. Because I know that all knowledge is available to me if I allow it to enter into my space, I seek and find answers to my challenges. I know that I know that I know. The universal abundance is mine and available to me this very moment.

This is my Divine Declaration.

Chapter Four

The Mind/Body/Spirit Connection

The Divine Declaration

"Health is a large word. It embraces not the body only, but the mind and spirit as well; . . . and not today's pain or pleasure alone, but the whole being and outlook of a man."
— James H. West

The Mind/Body/Spirit Connection

Considering how our emotions and thoughts affect our lives, we must also examine the mind/body/spirit connection. If the mind and spirit are in turmoil, the body responds in like manner, sometimes through *dis-ease*. Understanding the mind/body/spirit connection leads to greater harmony in all areas of our life.

MEDICAL RESEARCH

There is a vast body of work exploring the mind/body/spirit connection. There are also medical doctors who endorse this connection. Dr. Deepak Chopra, Dr. Andrew Weil, Dr. Gabor Maté, and Dr. John E. Sarno have written a wealth of material in this arena.

Dr. Weil encourages us to take charge of our health, physically, and mentally. He notes that the physical body is bombarded daily by various environmental elements including toxins in the air we breathe, the water we drink, the preservatives and various additives in our food, and even extreme weather conditions. Dr. Weil offers a program to minimize the effects of these environmental factors. In

The Divine Declaration

his book, *Spontaneous Healing*, Dr. Weil promotes changing our eating habits to a healthier diet by eliminating foods containing many chemicals and fats that are unhealthy, choosing organic foods when possible, and using a water filtration system for the tap water we drink. You may also consider placing an air filter in your home to enhance indoor air quality.

Dr. Weil shares anecdotes of people who are physically ill and explains the emotional disharmony connection to *dis-ease* in their bodies. His research signifies that stress is detrimental to the body, and that healing may occur after resolving an intolerable situation in your life. Interestingly, falling in love may be another avenue that promotes healing. He also suggests that releasing pent-up anger can prompt physical healing.

In Dr. Chopra's teachings, you find the mind/body/spirit connection in relation to physical health is paramount in healing, living longer, and living healthier. He teaches that the spiritual part of us, or who we really are, is vital to our physical health. If we awaken to our divine nature and move into thought patterns of believing in our powerful *Self*, we also change the physiological dynamics of our bodies. Understanding your divine nature and awakening to your Divine Inner Power impacts every aspect of your life.

Dr. Chopra encourages us to embrace our spiritual nature and choose from this aspect rather than from the ego. When we transition from placing intrinsic value in positions and possessions to establishing our worth in our spiritual nature, we create a different

The Mind/Body/Spirit Connection

life pattern. Once we recognize we want to live our purpose, rather than exist in status quo, this realization alters our physiology and body chemistry. We can strengthen our immune system through awareness of our talents and using them for the good of all. If we consciously choose to exercise and eat healthy foods, our choice can affect the health of our hearts and reduce high blood pressure. This may seem amazing at first glance, but if you examine how negative thoughts give rise to anger, sadness, or resentment, and how positive thoughts create excitement, joy, and the propensity to make great things happen in your life, it is logical. Our thoughts and choices affect our physical body as well as our mental health.

We can work emotionally and spiritually to help create better health. If you are living with health-related issues, it is helpful to remember stress is a major contributor to impaired health. According to an article by the American Academy of Family Physicians, "Your body responds to the way you think, feel, and act."

Examples of stress-related issues are high blood pressure and stomach ulcers. In addition, the following ailments may be signs in your physical body that your emotional health is out of balance: back pain, change in appetite, chest pain, constipation or diarrhea, dry mouth, fatigue, general aches and pains, headaches, insomnia, lightheadedness, palpitations (heart racing), shortness of breath, stiff neck, sweating, upset stomach, and weight gain or loss.

The article explains that compromised emotional health weakens the immune system and allows colds and infections easy entrance.

The Divine Declaration

It is beneficial to understand fully the role of stress in physical health. We all face stress in our daily lives, and it exacts its toll if we aren't able to break the cycle. In her article "Emotions and Disease," Ruth Levy Guyer, Ph.D., refers to Hans Selye, a Montreal physician who labeled a condition called "stress syndrome." According to Guyer, Selye concluded that in western cultures people are constantly exposed to stress, noise, and danger. People in these cultures experience overwhelming pressures, and are plagued with feelings of powerlessness and hopelessness. Stress is a constant in our lives to which we respond by remaining in the "on" position for days, months, or years. This response promotes stress syndrome and impacts us both physically and emotionally.

Stress also affects the balance of our body fluids and hormones, both of which are key to physical health. Guyer notes ancient physicians understood that if the following four fluids — phlegm, blood, black bile, and yellow bile — were not balanced, disease resulted. Health could only be restored when these fluids were balanced. She also states, today it is understood that balance "involving circulating molecules called interleukins, neurotransmitters, and hormones that send signals to each other…" needs to be maintained for optimal wellness. Experiencing intense, negative, or painful emotions triggers these chemical components and fuels momentum toward disease.

"The Mind Body Connection" article, published by the Calgary Health Region Learning and Development, supports this stress syndrome theory. When a person feels anxiety, anger, or fear, the body responds. The fight-or-flight response triggers an increase in heart rate, rapid breathing, and muscle tension. Occasional, short-term stress does not necessarily evolve into physical illness, but when we are stressed for greater periods of time, physical illness can result. This article reaffirms the Hans Selye theory that stress and anxiety are detrimental to the immune system, leaving the body vulnerable to illness.

I can see the results of how stress affects my own physical well-being. For example, childhood experiences may reside in various parts of the body. While working with an energy healer on my chronic neck pain, I have learned that blocked emotional energy or enduring emotional damage in childhood manifests in the body's power centers. My neck pain was a natural physical response to suppressed emotions. As a child, I was unable to express emotions because displays of anger or unhappiness could cost me a home. I was expected to endure and keep quiet about any pain or needs that I had. A social worker and one of my foster parents reminded me that I was lucky to have a roof over my head and food to eat, and I simply shouldn't expect anything more. This suppression created great stress in my life and led to chronic stomachaches during my third grade school year. Even now, when I am in a stressful situation and feel unable to express myself, I observe the neck pain and headache and seek to alleviate the emotional situation triggering this response.

Back and neck pain have a strong emotional component. I recently discovered Dr. John E. Sarno's body of work covering back pain. After reading his material and due to my strong belief in the mind/body/spirit connection, supported with MRI findings of only a slight interior bulge in the disc between my C5-C6 vertebrae, I have decided to delay seeing a neurosurgeon regarding my neck pain. As an alternative, I am working with a neurologist and continuing my work with an energy healer as the therapeutic modalities to release the physical and emotional pain.

In his books *Healing Back Pain* and *The MindBody Prescription*, Dr. Sarno shares valuable information regarding the psychological and physiological connection. Back and neck pain have reached epidemic proportions in America. Through his years of work with patients, he found most of them experienced a condition he termed TMS — Tension Myositis Syndrome. The group with the highest numbers of back pain fall between the ages 30 and 60, the years of work and responsibility.

Dr. Sarno explains that muscle tension and pain is rooted in anxiety, repressed anger, and suppressed emotions. His findings reveal that tension, not a spinal structural abnormality, is often the underlying cause of excruciating pain in many of his patients with back and neck pain. Just knowing that the condition is tension induced, rather than a frightening structural malady, is the jump start his program provides his patients on their path of living pain free. He instructs them to shift from thinking of the pain physically to a psychological position of working through and releasing their pain.

YOUR DIVINE INNER POWER AND WELL-BEING CONNECTION

Attitude is a vital component of health. You might ask, "What does happiness have to do with health?"

In answer to this question, observe people with positive attitudes who seem to be resilient to life's stresses and strains. Others without this resilience factor are more vulnerable to adversity, stress, and illness.

Like attitude, meditation and prayer influence healing. Meditation reduces stress and allows the mind a rest from the incessant thoughts crowding our psyche throughout the day. Most of us are whirling tops with thoughts of what we must do, what might happen, and what we should have done. Meditation is a time of pinpoint focus and brings us into the now, where we can access our inner power, learn to enjoy life, and live up to our highest potential.

In her article "Longevity May Have Spiritual Link," Paula J. Wart notes the power of the spirituality/health connection discovered through a Vanderbilt University study —

> *Researchers have found that healthy seniors who participate in private religious activity have an advantage when it comes to survival. Meditation, prayer, and other forms of spirituality have been associated with decreased mortality from heart and other diseases. Prayer, Bible study, meditation, and other forms of spiritual activity have been found to lower blood pressure....A number of studies have found positive medical benefits to meditation, possibly due to the body's reaction to reduced excretion of stress hormones,*

decreased heart rate and blood pressure, reduced oxygen consumption, and even changes in brain wave activity. Prayer appears to have similar benefits to Transcendental Meditation, mindfulness meditation, and chanting.

However, this research indicates that some medical experts are concerned with people blaming themselves for ill health and thinking they are not spiritual enough, "citing the fact that both spiritual and non-spiritual people become ill and die."

When you are working on physical healing, it is important not to get caught in blame and shame. Practicing meditation, prayer, and other forms of spirituality are methods for increasing awareness and tapping into your higher power and potential. They serve to provide you power in your life, not create a place for blame. These practices and healing modes are for your benefit.

INTEGRATIVE HEALING

EMDR is an effective modality for working through emotional pain. An energy healer and psychotherapist with whom I have worked has used EMDR (Eye Movement Desensitization and Reprocessing) to help me work through traumatic life events. EMDR involves either an eye movement model or a tapping model. The eye movement structure guides your eyes to follow lights horizontally across a light board and the tapping method is administered through holding a small electrode element between the thumb and index finger in each hand. During the process, I recalled traumatic events such as leaving my first foster home. The therapist helped me to explore my feelings and change how I emotionally processed this event. This technique helped me reconstruct the emotional framework I had built around that event. I had deep wounds from leaving my first foster home. I felt connected to my foster parents, so leaving them at age seven was one of the most traumatic events of my life. I found with each EMDR session I was a little less devastated than the prior session. After four sessions, I felt the pain was emotionally manageable.

To further facilitate physical and emotional healing, the energy healer/psychotherapist incorporated energy work and spiritual and cognitive counseling to work in concert with the EMDR. Energetic healing has been very effective for increasing my emotional and spiritual balance.

We are all energetic beings. Energy permeates the universe. This physical energetic process involves setting an intention for the healing, aligning and balancing the chakras, charging the energy fields immediately surrounding the physical body, and aligning the hara.

For a brief overview of energy healing, we will begin with the four dimensions of creative energies. According to Barbara Ann Brennan, author of *Light Emerging*, these four dimensions are the creative life forces. She explains, "…what they do, and how they function helps release your creative energies for health, healing or creating something new in your life….It is through life energy fields that your life situations, events, and experiences, as well as your material world, are created."

Brennan outlines four dimensions of this life force: the physical level, the auric level, the haric level, and the core star level.

The first dimension or the physical level is held in place by levels of energy and consciousness. The second level — the aura or auric energy field — lies just below the physical realm and is the foundation for the physical being. Our experience in the physical world was first on the auric level. Our feelings and personality reside in the auric field and are expressed through the physical body. For example, happiness gives rise to a smile.

The auric field is comprised of the following seven layers:

1. Physical sensation
2. Emotions with respect to self
3. Rational mind
4. Relations with others
5. Divine will within
6. Divine love, spiritual ecstasy
7. Divine mind, serenity

During an energy healing session, the energy healer clears and charges these seven fields, strengthening each layer in the process.

The chakras are also major components in energy healing. A healer works with seven chakras that relate to the seven layers in the auric field. In Sanskrit, *chakra* is a wheel. The healer works to balance the chakras in addition to healing the four life force levels. The chakras are energy centers aligned along the center of the body. When they are closed, the life force energy referred to as *chi* or *prana* energy in the eastern tradition, or *kundalini* energy in the Hindu tradition, is interrupted and causes disturbance in the whole person. The healer works to balance the chakras in an effort to allow the resurgence of energy to flow through these centers. According to Brennan's body of work, the seven chakras correspond to the seven layers of the field.

The Mind/Body/Spirit Connection

The first chakra is located at the sacral-coccyx joint at the base of the spine or between the legs. It relates to survival and is associated with kinesthetic (body position sense), proprioceptive (body movement), and tactile (touch) sense. It corresponds to our will to live and aids our physical energy. This chakra provides energy for the spinal column, the adrenal glands, and the kidneys.

The second chakra is located just above the pubic bone or just below the navel, and energy flows through the sacrum. It is through this chakra that we sense emotions. It also supplies our sexual organs and immune systems with life energy.

The third chakra is at the solar plexus or in the diaphragm area. It supplies the stomach, liver, gall bladder, pancreas, spleen, and nervous system with the necessary life force energy. It corresponds to our intuition and our connection with others, to who we are in the world, and to how we nurture ourselves.

The fourth chakra is located in the heart area and through this chakra we are able to feel love. This chakra supplies energy to the heart, circulatory system, thymus, vagus nerve, and upper back.

The fifth chakra is located in the throat and relates to hearing, taste, and smell. This chakra supplies energy to the thyroid, lungs, and alimentary canal. Speaking our truth and giving and receiving are the actions affiliated with this chakra.

The sixth chakra is located in the center of the forehead. This chakra provides energy to our pituitary gland, the lower brain, left eye, nose, ears, and nervous system. It relates to sight, conceptual understanding, and logistics of how we accomplish our ideas.

The seventh chakra is at the top of the head, or crown, and

supplies energy to our upper brain and right eye. It relates to tacit or direct knowing and to marrying the personality with spirituality.

The third field just below the auric level is the haric level. This level holds our intentions and is a considerable leap into our inner nature. The Japanese define the *hara* "as a center of power within the lower belly." This level is connected with our deeper life and spiritual purpose. Our intentions are critical in the creative process. If we are in conflict with our intentions, the creative process is blocked. When our intentions are in alignment, we are able to utilize this creativity. During the healing session, the hara is aligned prior to charging the auric energy fields.

The most center level and just below the haric level is the core star, which is our divinity residing inside of us. It is the divine part of us by which we are able to connect with God and access our Divine Inner Power. Brennan notes, it is from this source that "all creativity from within arises….It is the internal source of life within….Indeed, it is beyond the limitations of time, space, and belief. It is the individual aspect of the divine."

The core star is located on the center line of the body, one and one-half inches above the navel. This core is the basic nature of who we are. It is like a snowflake — each one is different. The core star represents the inner level from which we access our ageless wisdom, loving nature, and abundant courage. Barbara Brennan describes the core star as the following —

> *This inner essence has not really changed with time. No negative experiences have ever really tainted it. Yes, our reactions to negative experiences may have covered it, or shrouded it, but they have never*

really changed it. It is our most basic nature. It is the deeper goodness within each of us. It is who we really are. It is from this place that all our creative energies arise. It is the eternal fountainhead within each of us from which all our creations come.

Energy healing involves working with all of these levels and balancing the chakras. During this process of energy work, the energy will flow freely from the core star, up through the haric level, and through the auric field to our physical bodies to help create health and balance in our life. This process is what Brennan refers to as "light emerging."

The healer works with the energy on each level through a series of light touches to the body, allowing energy to flow into these areas and achieve balance. If these levels are blocked, we find pain in our life, which is our signal for change.

Youthing is another interesting process through which we can balance our chakras and increase our energy flow. Peter Kelder shares insightful information on this subject in his book, *Ancient Secrets of The Fountain of Youth*. According to Kelder, the secret to youth is found in a series of ancient Tibetan exercises or rites designed to "restore youthful health and vitality by balancing and harmonizing invisible energy vortexes within the body."

These rites can be performed in just a few minutes. Kelder refers to the chakras as seven energy vortexes and explains that these vortexes govern the endocrine system. He also notes how the energy flow through these centers affects the physical body. "When all seven energy vortexes are revolving at high speed, and at the same rate of speed, the body is in perfect health. When one or more of them slows down, aging and physical deterioration set in."

Therefore, we can see the importance of a balanced system of the body, mind, and spirit. For an in-depth understanding of how to perform the rites, you may want to review his book.

Kelder also addresses diet in the book and subscribes to a similar system of eating discussed in the book *Fit for Life*, by Harvey and Marilyn Diamond. Both works agree the food groups should be eaten separately. For example, they recommend that we abstain from mixing protein with starches and sugar. Vegetables can be eaten with either group, but we are instructed not to mix meat and potatoes or dessert. Starches cause the blood sugar to rise. The body responds by secreting insulin, which converts food to fat. Furthermore, our digestive systems require a different digestive fluid to digest meat than is needed to digest starch. When the foods are mixed in the stomach, the digestive tract breaks down the food more slowly than when food groups are eaten separately.

Another important point for optimum health is to remember to drink plenty of water because it keeps the body hydrated and helps flush toxins. Use a water filter to remove the chlorine and other elements in your drinking water. As an additional step for increasing healthy water use in your home, install a shower water filter to remove chlorine while showering.

When making choices in maintaining your physical health, consider all of your options, conventional and alternative. There is value in both. In researching the mind, body, spirit connection, I have found most of the research embraces moderation and balance. Balancing your emotions, spiritual life, and physical body is a rewarding and worthwhile endeavor. The choices lie within you.

The Mind/Body/Spirit Connection

Recognizing your Divine Inner Power will help you on your way in making better choices for your emotional, spiritual, and physical well-being. Take charge of your health. Connect to your Divine Inner Power, conduct the research, ask the questions, think you can, and pursue your options. Healing occurs every day. We know that our spiritual nature and mental attitude are tremendous factors impacting physical well-being.

The Divine Declaration IV—My Healthy Mind, Body, and Spirit

When in the course of my life, I find repression, unhappiness, ill-health, a chaotic state of mind, and a general sense of hopelessness, it is essential that I release any old programming, ties to the past, current situations, or people who are not supportive of my happiness, my ability to pursue my dreams, my general well-being, and my spiritual, emotional, and mental growth. I now assume my connection to God, the Divine Source, and recognize the power residing inside of me. I was created by the Divine Source; therefore, it must hold true that I am connected to this divinity and have access to a greater power. It is inside of me. It is my divine inheritance. I choose a new path of freedom from the albatross of unworthiness today. The weight is gone. A new world awaits me. And, so it is.

Thank you, Universe. Thank you, God.

The Mind/Body/Spirit Connection

I now accept as true and hold these truths to be evident: My emotional and spiritual thoughts are contributing to my physical health. I find it appealing to eat healthy foods. I choose an exercise I enjoy and make it a consistent part of my life. I take charge of my own health and make choices that reflect my inner power. I release any guilt surrounding my physical health. I know that my emotions affect my health, and guilt has no place here. It is with a sense of healing power that I assume responsibility for my health. I will now pursue the route of spiritual, emotional, and physical health. I am excited about moving forward in a direction that promotes my well-being. I will work to release any anger or fear I am holding as this release will free energy for a more positive outlook on life. I will work to resolve any situations in my life that are emotionally intolerable. I will take the steps in my life to know who I really am and explore my options to live up to my dreams and potential. I take this opportunity to heal my life, and I willingly go forth to experience my spiritual, emotional, and physical well-being.

This is my Divine Declaration.

Section Three

Experience and Expand Your Divine Inner Power

Chapter Five

How to Awaken To, Experience, and Expand Your Divine Inner Power

The Divine Declaration

"*Imagination is the beginning of creation. You imagine what you desire, you will what you imagine and at last you create what you will.*"
— George Bernard Shaw

How to Awaken To, Experience, and Expand Your Divine Power

Most of us manage change in our lives with greater ease if we have a plan. With a map or program to follow, we can begin our journey and set our course. When I attended sailing ground school, I used a reference book to help me learn the knots, parts of the boat, and rules of the water. It is beneficial to have instructions for reference when you're embarking on a new adventure or any endeavor for which you haven't yet mastered. I have mapped out a powerful course for you. It will help you to awaken to, experience, and expand your Divine Inner Power. Through the Divine Inner Power Connection Paths in this chapter, you can change your life. These paths include:

1. Meditation. Meditation is a process that helps you calm your mind and allows spiritual rejuvenation. It creates space for divine universal information to rise and flow.

2. Affirmative Prayer. Affirmative prayer is praying in the positive. It is a method of praying with faith, knowing that your desire is founded in the realm of possibilities. It is also knowing that you wouldn't have the desire if it were impossible to attain.

3. Creative Visualization. Creative visualization is a method of seeing through your mind's eye what helps to calm your mind or what you wish to create in your life.
4. Treasure Mapping. Treasure mapping is a technique that places your desires in physical form. It is a creative process that helps you clearly define your desires through pictures and the written word.
5. Journaling. Journaling is the practice of writing and releasing old programming and energy, and recording and creating new goals and possibilities for your life.

Each process is active and keeps us sharply focused on what we need to do to bring about the life changes we are seeking. Like a backup generator, when your connection to your divine nature dims, the creative igniters covered in this chapter will spark your Divine Inner Power flame.

MEDITATION

The objective of meditation is to relax and open your mind, to give it a break by relinquishing the attachment to your thoughts as they pass. Meditation creates a space of silence and spiritual awakening. Deepak Chopra refers to the space between your thoughts as the "gap." Connecting with your Divine Inner Power requires that you take time to clear the embedded, suppressive, and negative subconscious programming. Once this old programming is released, you fill this void with new inspirational information through the Divine Inner Power Connection Paths.

Meditation clears your thoughts, calms your mind, and suspends the chatter. It is much like a gentle rain after the storm. It is a cleansing, peaceful feeling, a restful place to create space for new divine inspirations and ideas to grow. We rest our bodies at night and our minds feel rejuvenated from a rest as well. When you reach the "gap" between your thoughts, you will desire that experience again.

First, let's clear away the debris. You may use any of these methods to empty the landfill in your mind. This process clears the way for the new programming. It doesn't simply cover the old programming with new material. These methods are designed to replace the old thought patterns stunting your growth and keeping you in the quicksand of unhappiness and dismay. Copy these pages and clip the programs, place or rewrite them on a card, and carry them with you to remind you of your greatness and the potential you are unlocking on this magnificent journey.

To begin the meditation process, you may choose to listen to calming music or soothing sounds of nature to enhance your relaxation as you experience your Divine Inner Power Connection Paths, or you may practice in silence.

You can meditate in a variety of positions. You may assume the lotus position, sitting flat with your legs crossed and your spine straight with shoulders relaxed. You may also sit in a chair with your spine straight and shoulders relaxed, or lie down with your back flat and spine straight (although lying down may be more challenging because we tend to fall asleep). Keeping the spine straight and vertical allows the divine energy (chi or kundalini energy) to flow through the chakras easily. Keeping the back straight also allows for deep breathing. Begin with 3 to 5 minute sessions, eventually working up to 20 or 30 minute sessions twice a day. You will also find brief meditation sessions are refreshing breaks from stress during the day. To experience an effective meditation session and allow your mind a break from incessant thoughts, follow the process outlined below:

Step 1: Keep your spine straight and vertical and allow your shoulders to relax.

Step 2: Breathe deeply five to ten times and allow your body to relax.

Step 3: Start counting along with your breathing. Count to four as you inhale and hold for a count of four. Then exhale for a count of four. This provides you a focal point, something on which to center your mind.

Step 4: Repeat the breathing exercise five to ten times, allowing your thoughts to flow through your mind. See your thoughts like floats in a parade: some beautiful, some just okay, and some difficult to look at. Just let them go down the street, and soon they will be out of sight. Or, see them as ripples on a pond after a tossed pebble has disturbed the calm, clear water. Watch the ripples disappear as they extend from the center.

Step 5: Let your thoughts go; don't analyze them. Simply observe them objectively. This release is a pivotal point of your meditation process. After the release process, you may use the following visualization for rejuvenation.

Step 6: Allow the divine light to enter into your crown chakra (at the top of your head) and flow through your body to fill every cell. See the white or white/golden light fill the cells of your body as it travels from the crown chakra down through your torso and through all of your physical body extending to your fingers and toes. Allow the light to flow out through your heart chakra and into the world as a rainbow light or send rainbow hearts of love or solid color hearts of love out into the universe.

As you relax into your deep meditation, enjoy what you are experiencing. Allow your thoughts to pass through without attachment. Let them go and calm your mind, opening the channel connected with the divine part of you. Your mind's clutter is released, creating open space for new information to flow into your consciousness.

If you feel angry or frustrated, send an orange ray of light out through the bottom of your feet and into the Earth as a grounding technique, then visualize the same light ray coming up from the earth as rainbow light transformed into new vibrant energy.

You may also use the violet flame as a purification of negative energy. Just as a ray of sunlight passing through a prism refracts into seven colors, spiritual light also divides into seven colors, or rays. Each ray has its own divine qualities. The violet flame, which originates from the violet ray, encompasses mercy, forgiveness, freedom, and transmutation. The color violet has traditionally been connected with spirituality. Violet has the highest frequency in the visible spectrum and is at the point of transition to the next light wave. The violet flame is a useful tool for self-transformation and is symbolic in spiritual transformation.

Visualize the violet flame inside of you. See it purifying your entire being, every cell, and the energy surrounding your physical

The Divine Declaration

body. Both of these techniques work well when you're working to release negative energy.

PREPARING FOR AFFIRMATIVE PRAYERS

The clearing techniques listed below help you open your energy to receive the Divine Inner Power Connection Paths that follow. Use these or revise them and create your own. During the clearing process, allow yourself to feel the release and relaxation. Give yourself the time you deserve to enjoy this rejuvenation experience and adventure.

CLEARING TECHNIQUES

Violet Waterfall of Divine Cleansing and Love

Sitting in the lotus position (or in whatever meditation position is most effective), close your eyes or focus on a candle or any fixed object with which you are able to connect. Slowly relax your toes, feet, ankles, calves, knees, thighs, hips, abdomen, chest, fingers, arms, shoulders, neck, face, and scalp. Feel the relaxation at each point of your body. Once you have allowed your body to relax, inhale deeply to the count of four, then hold your breath to the count of four, and exhale to the count of four. Practice this breathing count several times.

Now, visualize a violet waterfall continuously flowing through your crown chakra and down through your body, cleansing your old mental constructs and the cells of your body as it flows. Recognize this as God's divine love flowing through you and feel the joy as this powerful energy moves through your body, permeating and rejuvenating every cell in your physical body with love and light.

Pristine Shower of Divine Cleansing and Love

Imagine yourself walking through a wide shower of pure, pristine water rinsing off all negativity and "hazardous waste" that has accumulated on you over the years. See this brilliant shimmering water seeping into your cells as the <u>divine love of God, cleansing and refilling each cell with love and light.</u>

Sacred Environment of Divine Cleansing and Love

Think of a beautiful sacred space where you feel secure and at peace. This may be a beautiful meadow, a beach, a forest, or a room in a house. If the setting is outside, see the sunshine surrounding you and beaming in through your crown chakra. Envision the rays brightly shining through your body, cleansing your energy and every cell with God's divine love. See the brilliant rays refilling you with love and light. If your sacred space is inside a building, visualize the light from a candle flame, a lamp, or even the sun shining through the windows. If you prefer a rainy day, see the rain as the shower rinsing off the negativity and "hazardous waste" as in the Pristine Shower above.

When you feel relaxed and have released any negativity, even for a few moments, use the following Divine Inner Power Connection Path prayers. These affirmative prayers reprogram your belief system and recharge your life with divine energy.

Remember what Jesus said to his disciples in St. Luke 11.9-10 —

And I say unto you, Ask, and it shall be given you; seek and ye shall find; know, and it shall be opened unto you. For every one that

The Divine Declaration

asketh receiveth; and he that seeketh findeth; and to him that knocketh it shall be opened.

The next few pages explore recharging your life in the areas of your well-being, relationships, health, and abundance. Remember that your belief system is your blueprint for building your life. Your core beliefs provide the outline and guidance for living, and you may make changes and re-design your life at any time during the process. Even if you feel your life is already "built" and set in place, you have the option to re-model the existing belief system and create a new life.

You may use the following programs as they are, or revise them and write your own programs tailored specifically to your life issues. Remember when designing your own programs, keep them positive and FEEL. Don't just think or visualize; feel what it would be like to already have what you would like to have in your life. For example, if you desire a new car, visualize yourself in the driver's seat and feel the excitement as if the car were already yours. Allow yourself to experience how you feel when you take the keys from the salesperson to drive the car home. Experience how it handles, smell the new car smell, see the interior and exterior color of the car, feel your hands on the steering wheel, and listen to the radio or your favorite CD. See yourself driving the car home and parking it in your garage. This exercise is an example of the specifics for feeling what you want to manifest.

How to Awaken To, Experience, and Expand Your Divine Power

AFFIRMATIVE PRAYER – DIVINE INNER POWER CONNECTION PATHS

After you relax and your mind is calm, and after any thought debris is released, say an ==affirmative prayer.== This prayer plants the seed of your desire. ==You pray with the faith that the outcome will be in your highest good.== We may not always immediately recognize what is in our highest good, so do not limit God and the Universe with attachment to a specific item, person, or desired path. Keep an open mind. Know that you are a divine spark of God, and that God wants you to be happy, reach your potential, and live your dreams in alignment with your highest good.

The following Affirmative Prayers are more effective steps on your path. You may also create your own specific paths for your life dreams.

Prayer One

I am a divine being of light. God wants me to be happy, healthy, peaceful, and live in abundance. I am a divine expression of God, the great divine being. I have a light that shines brightly and illuminates my path. Thank you, Universe. Thank you, God, Divine Source, All that is. Amen.

Prayer Two

I focus on my life dreams, and they manifest through me in divine right timing and divine order. I trust in the law of manifestation — that what I focus on I create more of in my life. I know that God wants my best, and I align my desires with my highest self for my greatest good. Thank you, Universe. Thank you, God, Divine Source, All that is. Amen.

The Divine Declaration

Prayer Three

I am grateful for the abundance I currently have in my life (list a few things for which you are grateful). As I focus on the abundance I have in my life now, I create more abundance. As I look around at the beauty of our universe — the trees, grass, mountains, flowers, stars, all the wildlife, the sea, the lakes, rivers and streams, and the great vast blue sky and universe beyond — I know I am home among this tremendous abundance and grandeur. Everything is part of this universal splendor, and I am equal to all of life's beauty and joy. Like attracts like, and I am connected to what I want to bring into my life. I am connected to the entire universe, and I open my lines of communication and magnetic attraction to draw to me my life's dreams and wishes. I attract opulence, true friends, health, and happiness into my life. As I follow my path, I am guided and directed to my highest and greatest good. I look at myself and others with love and compassion because I know we are all doing the best we can at this time. I look toward the light, and as I evolve spiritually, I help bring the whole planet's vibration to a higher level. I am thankful for this opportunity. Thank you, Universe. Thank you, God, Divine Source, All that is. Amen.

Prayer Four

I am love, loving and loved. I attract loving and supporting relationships in my life. I connect only with what contributes to my life in a positive and supportive way. I release all things hindering my happiness, spiritual growth, self-love, and ability to expand. I have room only for love, peace, happiness, health, and expansion. I sit quietly and know my divine connection and smile at this realization. Thank you, Universe. Thank you, God, Divine Source, All that is. Amen.

Prayer Five

I keep a positive outlook, even in the midst of adversity. When negative energy is around me, I realign with my divinity. This realignment fills me with warmth and love and lifts me to believe in my dreams and see beyond the immediate horizon. Like a bird whose wing is broken, I will heal from inside and fly again. Flying is what I do best, and I will soar. Thank you, Universe. Thank you, God, Divine Source, All that is. Amen.

These Affirmative Prayers help you get in touch with your divine nature and Divine Inner Power. If feeling your abundance in the now moment is challenging, I recommend that you continue practicing the relaxation techniques and gradually move into the visualization exercises. Feeling that you already have what you desire, coupled with the visualization, provides a powerful component in the process. If you encounter resistance or difficulty connecting with your desire, you might ask yourself a question to get in touch with your feelings and desire more deeply. For example, you could ask, "Why do I want this?" In answer, search beyond the superficial reasons and uncover the core. This mental examination brings you to a focal point where you can ask yourself, "How would I feel with this right now?"

Reprogramming our thought patterns is one of the most productive ways to reclaim our power. These paths are not just rhetoric; they are new ways of looking at your life. We choose our life perception every day, every moment, and we can change it at any moment. Why not look for ways and means of happiness instead of despair?

Reprogramming for a positive outlook and happiness doesn't mean you disregard grief, sadness, or anger. However, it does mean allowing yourself to feel deeply and then to move through the emotion, processing it along the way. When a baby feels pain, the child doesn't suppress the feeling and redirect it as rage or violence. Instead, the child fully acknowledges the pain, screams, or cries, and moves on. This emotional process is a very useful way to work with our anger and grief. It is necessary to understand our repressed anger and its origination point. In moving through our anger and grief, we do not forget. We just do not linger indefinitely. We recognize the pain or anger, process it, and free our energy for our greater purpose.

CREATIVE VISUALIZATION

Creative visualization is another powerful tool in the spiritual toolbox to expand your Divine Inner Power. Daydreaming is a form of creative visualization without discipline, but we will explore a disciplined form of visualization to help you with your inner journey of manifestation.

To unleash your soul's potential power, visualize what you want as if it already exists. Remember to see the end results. Don't get caught in the details. Your subconscious mind will register your feelings and connection to the end result. No need to worry or fret about the how, why, when, or where; your Divine Inner Power will work to take you to the heights of your dreams. For instance, picture yourself working at that new job you want as if you already have the job. In her book *Creative Visualization*, Shakti Gawain, explains this process —

How to Awaken To, Experience, and Expand Your Divine Power

In creative visualization you use your imagination to create a clear image, idea, or feeling of something you wish to manifest. Then you continue to focus on the idea, feeling, or picture regularly, giving it positive energy until it becomes objective reality...in other words, until you actually achieve what you have been imagining.

I recommend that you practice manifesting creative visualization each day. You may focus twice a day for 5 to 15 minutes on your desire, or you may want to maintain clear focus for 17 seconds three times a day. This clear, 17-second focus is powerful. It equals hours of physical effort in working toward your desire. After you practice the visualization, release your desire to allow the creative energy to support your desire and let it filter down to the physical level. You may surround it in white light and release it like a hot air balloon, allowing it to connect with the universal energy, attracting positive energy as it ascends. Passionate visualization with intense affirmative feeling is one of the most effective ways to manifest.

Remember when working with creative visualization to stay in affirmative energy. If you encounter fear or frustration around your desire, get to the root of it, and work through what is troubling you and may be blocking the desire. You may have feelings of unworthiness that you need to change in order to clear the path for your desire to manifest. Or, you may have been taught that life is full of suffering. This core belief may be hindering your acceptance that you can have a life of happiness and abundance, but you can move through the fear and frustration. Working with a counselor to release the emotional block may prove helpful in this process. Connecting with your Divine Inner Power opens your relationship with God,

The Divine Declaration

which is based on infinite love. As you work with manifesting, reinforce your belief system that God wants your highest good. Align your energy and heart with God and your highest good. You deserve the best!

You may prefer to enter your sacred space through meditation prior to working with these visualizations, or you may work directly with the visualization technique. Work with your own personally designed visualizations, or try one of the following examples:

Romantic Relationship Visualization

If a romantic relationship is what you desire, see yourself with a mate. If you are not romantically involved with someone right now, simply see and feel the connection of a partner. See the two of you holding hands, walking through the forest, or strolling on a beach. Feel what it is like to have someone love you completely. You trust this person. It is a warm feeling inside. See the wedding band on your finger. What does that feel like? See you and your partner during the holidays together, enjoying the splendid moments. Enjoy your favorite activities with this person. Enjoy the hugs and kisses. See the end results. Do not get caught in the details of how. Know that Divine Source and universal energy supports your heart's desires. End the visualization with the statement: *This or something better — my highest good is manifesting now.*

Life Purpose or Bliss Visualization

See yourself engaged in your dream profession or purpose. Visualize yourself in the day-to-day activities of this dream life. What skills do you have, where do you conduct this activity, and how does it feel while you are engaged in this purpose? Stay with this feeling for a few minutes, fully experiencing how it feels to have this opportunity. See the end results, do not get caught in the details of how, and know that Divine Source and universal energy support your heart's desires. End the visualization with the statement: *This or something better — my highest good is manifesting now.*

Physical Health Visualization

See your physical body as whole and properly functioning. Your body is in divine order, healthy and vital. Through divine eyes, all is perfect in divine order. Your organs, muscles, skeletal system, endocrine system, and central nervous system are all functioning properly and keeping you healthy and alive. You are strong and healing more and more every day. You now feel energetic and healthy. Pain is non-existent. You now feel healthy where there was pain. You now feel joy where there was pain or dysfunction in your physical body. Allow a few minutes for this feeling to sink in. See the end results, do not get caught in the details of how, and know that Divine Source and universal energy supports your heart's desires. End the visualization with the statement: *This or something better — my highest good is manifesting now.*

Financial Abundance

See yourself with abundant financial security. You have the financial means to live the life you desire. There is no lack in the universe, only a thought system created on the physical plane. Open your heart and mind to your abundance now. See your financial picture growing more and more healthy day-by-day. Visualize your reaction to how great it feels to know that the universe supports you in your abundance. See the abundance all around you that is already manifested on the physical plane. The stars, the sky, the ocean, and the sun are great examples of abundance. Abundance is all around you! Accept this abundance; replace your small dipper with a large vessel to fill with abundance from the universal well. Go and claim your share! Know that Divine Source and universal energy supports your heart's desires. End the visualization with the statement: *This or something better — my highest good is manifesting now.*

A meditation guide, such as a hypnotherapist or counselor, can help you proceed in this endeavor if you are having difficulty seeing or feeling your desire. A meditation guide can help you with guided visualization and combine it with feeling for powerful results. Writing or creating your own visualization is quite workable, too. Keep in mind that feeling the emotion attached to the visualization brings it significant power. If it is difficult for you to feel, ask yourself questions about why you want this desire in your life and how it will impact you. Let God or the Divine Source and your Divine Inner Power take care of the details. Focus on the end result. Again, to reiterate, don't get bogged down in the details of how it will come to be. Your subconscious mind doesn't discern between real and imagined, so imagine your desire already in physical or spiritual form. End the visualization exercise with a statement similar to "This or something better is happening in my life now." This statement does not lock your happiness into a specific person or event, but it allows space for your highest good to take form.

Using creative visualization in conjunction with the affirmative prayer experience discussed earlier in this chapter is an effective, workable approach. Include your visualizations with your affirmative prayer programs. Record an audio version of your affirmative prayers and visualizations and listen to it when you're ready for sleep. This encourages the process in your subconscious mind while your conscious thoughts are resting and out of your way.

To begin, follow the same procedure as the affirmative prayer by relaxing and getting into the allow mode. As soon as you are in the allow mode, your inner power can work its magic through the law of the universe. Place yourself in your own sanctuary, which may be in a meadow, on a cloud, out in space, in a boat on the ocean, in your bedroom, or any room in your home. Most important is that you feel safe, secure, and peaceful in your sanctuary. See it clearly in your mind's eye, then roll your life film and enjoy!

LIFE TREASURE MAPPING

Life treasure mapping is another creative, enjoyable, and active step to connect with your Divine Inner Power. Your Life Treasure Map is symbolic of what you desire and wish to manifest. Treasure mapping works well because it concretely establishes a visual platform of your life's desires. There it is in black and white and in color, a hard copy of your dreams. The pages stir excitement in your soul by representing your new life. It is the process of surveying, blueprinting, and building your dream in a symbolic, artistic manner.

Remember cut & paste in art class? Similar to art class in elementary school, life treasure mapping is fun, except it will have a powerful impact on your path of creating your reality through your inner power. This process involves your focus on several levels. Find photos, words, and symbols that represent what you would like to create in your life and paste them thematically in a scrap book of your choice. You may want a title on your book or cover it with material and make it a real treasure. A poster will also work well because you can display it and see it every day. You may choose to design both a scrap book and a poster.

My Life Treasure Map is divided into theme pages: an opening section, life purpose, divine right relationship and family, and home environments that I would like for my life. I have found words, phrases, and photos exemplifying what I desire. I found many representations of my life desires in magazines and books.

On the left page of my opening section is the lone word *hope*. I found this word in a magazine that resembles the handwriting of a child. The right-hand page features a phrase cut out from a magazine, and it reads, *Well within your reach.*

The next section is dedicated to my Divine Inner Power and life purpose. It is filled with inspirational quotes and photos: *Create the life you've always wanted, A stunning novel of spiritual awakening by the best-selling author, INSTANT MEMORY, You are greater than you think!, The Blessings of Abundance, Woman Deserves The Best!, Healing from Within, Reaching for the Skies,* and a photo of a beautiful floral and lace dress. I even found my last name printed in a magazine and pasted it several times on the pages.

The next three pages represent my divine-right relationship and family life. Examples from this section include: *When my youngest foster daughter announced her long-awaited wedding plans* (Wow, how specific!); a photo of a puppy eating ice cream from a silver spoon with the caption, *Careful, or next he'll expect to be carried on walks* (again, I felt quite a connection to this photo); a sticker that states, *Something wonderful is about to happen*; photos of pearls and quotes of love.

The next three pages are filled with photos of and quotes about my dream home and property. They include interior and exterior home photos. I dream of living in the countryside, so there are pictures of breathtaking landscapes of pastures, flowers, rolling hills, gardens and a woman picking flowers in a meadow. Some of the notable quotes read: *A Place to Call Home, Quality Worth Coming Home To, Tending to Your Dreams, A Countryside of Dreams,* and *Being Put Out to Pasture Isn't So Bad, As Long As You Own The Pasture.*

The next page reflects my interest in sailing and the ocean, with photos of boats and a few quotes. One in particular that stirs my soul is, *Down harbour, round the point, was the open sea. Here was the freedom I desire, long sought-for, not yet known. Freedom to write, to walk, to wander, freedom to climb hills, to pull a boat, to be alone.* (From *Enchanted Cornwall* by Daphne du Maurier)

I enjoyed creating this project, and I hope it will be as delightful for you. Below are the materials you will need to begin mapping your desires.

Either purchase a scrap book or make one with a photo album you have at home. You also need a glue stick, scissors, some of your favorite magazines and newspapers, and photos of yourself, your feathered, furry, and non-furry children, and whatever else you would like to include in your Life Treasure Map.

Locate and clip words, phrases, and photos of what you desire for your life purpose: home, divine right relationship, family or children — feathered, furry, and non-furry. Choose images that depict healthy living, vacation, or retirement property and any specific item such as a car, house, or other passion. Fashion them on the page. Some may overlap others, and photos and words may point in different directions.

After you have completed some of the pages, go back and look at these pages as often as you can. When looking at a hard copy of your desires, you will feel divine. The feeling, coupled with the thought and visualization of already having what you want in your life, is creating your dreams for you in spirit and it eventually filters into the physical realm.

JOURNALING

Journaling is yet another powerful way to focus your energy on manifesting your desires. Writing what you desire in the affirmative, like the affirmative prayer, is a pinpoint focus for your Divine Inner Power manifestations. Journaling helps you set your desires in motion in much the same way the treasure mapping does. Journaling consists of writing the pages of your life's desires. Some people prefer this writing technique and already keep a journal. As Richard Bach tells us in his book, *Illusions*, we are free to write our life script: "The world is your exercise book, the pages on which you do your sums. It is not reality, although you can express reality there if you wish. You are also free to write nonsense, or lies, or to tear the pages."

For our purpose, this journaling is inspirational. Write in your exercise book inspirational quotes from books or notes of what others share with you. You may even write a "purchase order to God and the universe." This purchase order is similar to affirmative prayer

How to Awaken To, Experience, and Expand Your Divine Power

in the written form. Write your desire as if you already have it. Add your gratitude by thanking God and the Universe in advance for your desire already in form. Writing goals is key to achieving them, and this power works the same with your manifestation process.

Use these techniques daily with focus, then release the energy to the divine support system of God, the Divine Source, and the Universe. Do not fret about the outcome. Go about your life in a productive manner. All is in divine right timing and divine right order.

Set aside time to exercise your Divine Inner Power just as you do to exercise physically. It is important to feed your life a steady diet of healthy spiritual and mental nourishment. We eat food for physical nourishment. We connect with our Divine Inner Power for life nourishment.

The Divine Declaration V – Experiencing and Expanding My Divine Inner Power

When in the course of my life, I find repression, unhappiness, ill-health, a chaotic state of mind, and a general sense of hopelessness, it is essential that I release any old programming, ties to the past, current situations, or people who are not supportive of my happiness, my ability to pursue my dreams, my general well-being, and my spiritual, emotional, and mental growth. I now assume my connection to God, the Divine Source, and recognize the power residing inside of me. I was created by the Divine Source; therefore, it must hold true that I am connected to this divinity and have access to a greater power. It is inside of me. It is my divine inheritance. I choose a new path of freedom from the albatross of unworthiness today. The weight is gone. A new world awaits me. And, so it is.

Thank you, Universe. Thank you, God.

How to Awaken To, Experience, and Expand Your Divine Power

I now accept as true and hold these truths to be evident: I am in charge of my life. Beginning today, I will do the things that will elevate my life. I will do at least one thing that is encouraging and inspirational. I am in awe of the universal abundance that surrounds me. I am an heir to this abundance. I need not fret or manipulate, nor become anxious about where or how my abundance will take form. I need only to connect with the Divine Source and know what I want for my life. It is through this divine connection that I access my abundance. My divine inner power will direct me toward my dreams. I will listen and take the steps toward greater fulfillment. I will spend time connecting to my divinity and strengthening my divine inner power. I pursue my dreams with excitement and take time to bring them to fruition. As I develop and connect with the real me, my life changes in positive ways. I am able to focus on what I want in life and take the steps to make it happen. I know it is up to me. I will love myself on this journey. I am worthy, I am loved, I am loving, and I am love.

This is my Divine Declaration.

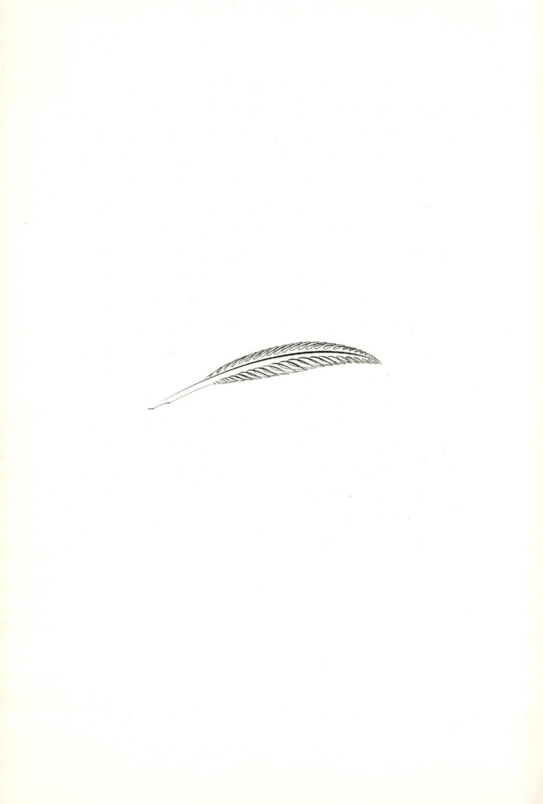

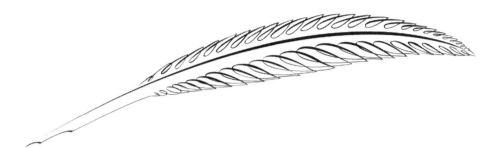

Chapter Six

Your Support System

The Divine Declaration

Piglet sidled up to Pooh from behind. "Pooh!" he whispered.

"Yes, Piglet?"

"Nothing," said Piglet, taking Pooh's paw. "I just wanted to be sure of you."

— A.A. Milne

Your Support System

Have you thought of how you relate to the people in your inner circle? Spiritual author John Harricharan once told me, "Be careful who you choose to be with most of the time, because you will become like them."

There are several proverbs along this line as well: "Water seeks its own level; Birds of a feather flock together; You'll know them by the company they keep; Like attracts like." On closer examination, these proverbs are quite accurate. Are the people with whom you keep close company supportive of who you are and secure within themselves? Are they generous with their compassion, kindness, and ability to express their love or are they guarded, rude, ridiculing, insecure, and unsupportive?

Exploring our external support system, internalizing that support, and understanding how we process our environment and direct our path is essential to building a life led by Divine Inner Power. Similar to a support beam in a house, our support system reinforces our life. You can construct a house without supports, but it may collapse in stressful conditions. You can build your life without others, but supportive people definitely enhance your life. My goal is to illustrate how support systems affect us, and how the internalization of our environment substantially directs our lives. Use this book as a support beam for your life as you tap into your Divine Inner Power.

First, closely examine your attitude and feelings about yourself and about the world to see if the people in your environment reflect those same attitudes and feelings. We attract different people into our lives based on where we are spiritually, emotionally, and mentally at the time. When I was sixteen, I attracted a relationship with a man who needed direction and who I thought needed someone to save him, to nurture him, someone to basically raise him. So at nineteen, I married him and tried to do that. After the relationship ended, I learned the nurturing efforts I projected onto my partner were actually the emotional dynamics I needed to heal my own wounds. At this point, I embarked on an inner journey to save myself. Sometimes, even now, I attempt to save other people and direct them, but this need occurs less frequently as I gain greater spiritual and emotional awareness. I now understand we must choose personal growth ourselves. No one can force us to quench our unfulfilled inner longings.

At this point in my life, I would not be attracted to a co-dependent relationship. Now I find I am interested in people who are working on their spirituality, seeking greater awareness, and who care about themselves and the world around them. I am quite a different person than I was at nineteen.

Your Support System

EXTERNAL SUPPORT

Many supportive people fill my life, and I am eternally grateful to them. When we are on our spiritual journeys, having a mentor or at least one person to support us is one of the most treasured relationships. This someone who genuinely cares, who is our cheerleader, or who helps guide us through rough waters, is also someone who celebrates with us when we have wind in our sails and calm water under our boats. This relationship is an asset with worth beyond measure.

While a supportive and nurturing environment is a critical component of coping and success, we must look inside and connect with our Divine Inner Power. We must find our own inner support and self-worth. To grow, flourish, and to allow and appreciate the support of others is like a plant thriving on sunshine and water. Ultimately, like the plant, we must utilize the nutrients to our fullest potential — it is an inside job.

Even Hollywood stars and famous musicians, when receiving an award, thank those who have supported them along the way. In their article, "I'd Like to Thank…," authors Ron Rubin and Stuart Avery Gold tell us —

> *On a planet populated with dream-killers, you must shelter yourself with the help of dream-livers, those kindred spirits who will support you in your desire to grow and assist in keeping your dreams from getting ground in the dust.*

It is important to surround yourself with supportive people who encourage you to live your dreams. Not simply "yes men," but people who genuinely support you and believe in you, your dreams, and your potential. We can always find someone who is a naysayer, but

The Divine Declaration

the naysayer is only regurgitating what is inside of them, not what is inside of you. Remember what Rubin and Gold have to say —

Do everything you can to attach yourself to nurturing, affirming people who have a positive mind, provide a positive push, who in good times and bad believe in your talents, passions, and dreams, having no doubt that you will one day WOW-ify the world with your accomplishments.

I can certainly think of those who have believed in me and my writing, even when I questioned my ability and promise. These people have helped me through the writing of this book and encouraged me to look forward to the next one. I can say, first hand, our support system is one of our greatest assets in life. When we couple this support with our Divine Inner Power, we will WOW-ify this world.

If we can accept this support and utilize it as literally "the wind beneath our wings," we will increase our altitude. It is you who must decide to fly, but support from others can help make the journey an exciting adventure.

My sister sent me a cute, but quite profound, allegory about an eagle and chickens. The gist of it was that chickens peck around on the ground and don't fly like eagles. Therefore, if you want to fly like an eagle, don't stay among the chickens because their life construct may affect your beliefs. It was appropriately titled "Chickens Can't Fly."

How important is it to maintain supportive relationships and release those that are vexations to our life? In college, my Spiritual Iconography professor told our class that it is imperative that we release relationships that tax us emotionally or spiritually. He said, "If a person isn't contributing to your spiritual, physical, or emotional well being, get away from them. I don't care if it is your child, a spouse, a parent, or a friend. If they are hindering your development simply get away from them."

He didn't mean this for children who are not of age. He wasn't promoting runaways, but he did want adults to assess their personal relationships.

INTERNAL SUPPORT - RESILIENCE AND INTERNAL LOCUS OF CONTROL

In another college psychology class, I researched the concepts of Resilience and Internal Locus of Control. I found both studies to be interesting and quite profound. Our internal locus of control is how we handle the situations that impact our lives, ultimately how we support ourselves. Resilience is how we rebound from adversity and return to our inner power and support. In other words, it is how we play the cards we are dealt rather than folding immediately. Playing out our hand, like anything else, is a skill. We can learn and practice until we eventually put up our chips and win the hand.

Resilience is the protective factor in individuals who are able to survive extreme adversity without personal destruction. Resilient individuals not only cope, but are able to flourish after enduring tremendous life challenges. Family counseling studies are now looking at not only how individuals survive, but also at how some people actually blossom in spite of adverse conditions they have faced.

Internal locus of control is a significant factor in developing resilience; it is also a protective factor. Internal locus of control is how we use our inner determination, self-direction, and self-motivation. If

The Divine Declaration

we have a strong internal locus of control, we accept responsibility for our decisions and our life.

The study of resilience examines an array of factors such as personality characteristics, attachment issues, level of social support, and the life stressors an individual endured that may have fostered resilience. Individual resilience grows through the support of others during childhood and continues into adulthood. This support can be found in parents, mentors, siblings, teachers, peers, and inspirational books.

We all know how great it feels to have someone support us emotionally when we pursue our dreams, are excited about a new adventure, worried about work issues, are physically ill, or feel disappointed or sad. Often, when we are ill, for example, we want our mother to care for us. We associate a mother's love with nurturing, and this support often helps us feel better.

Think of how you feel when someone you love congratulates you on a job well done, or how you felt as a child when someone stepped in to help with your homework or a difficult project you had tackled. Perhaps someone listened with a compassionate ear to your sad story of the break up of a romantic relationship. Even in professional sports, the team has cheerleaders to support and fuel the excitement of the game. Physically and mentally ill individuals have health support groups. Teams of researchers support each other, and ground control supports the NASA astronauts.

The following are resilience protective factors or characteristics belonging to the individual that reduce the effect of stressful encounters and problems:

Your Support System

> Is able to give of self in order to help others and/or support a cause
> Uses healthy life skills, such as responsible decision making
> Is assertive or confident in interactions with others
> Uses impulse control, able to delay gratification
> Is able to solve problems, has critical thinking capacity
> Is able to be a friend and forms positive relationships
> Has a sense of humor
> Utilizes internal locus of control
> Is perceptive to the signals from others
> Is autonomous/independent
> Has a positive view of personal future
> Is flexible regarding change
> Has the capacity for and interest in learning
> Has the ability to follow through
> Is self-motivated, develops talent and personal competence
> Has a feeling of self-worth and self-confidence
> Values integrity
> Has faith in something greater than the physical or believes in God or Divine Source

What causes one individual to choose a productive life, and another to choose a less desirable lifestyle, when both have faced adversity or lived in the same environment? In comparison, what is the determinant that causes people to achieve great success and rise

The Divine Declaration

out of poverty, compared to others who were privileged and live a life of mediocrity and quiet desperation?

Resilience and internal locus of control play critical roles in our emotional health. Having a sense of our inner power, working for what we want in life, taking steps toward our goals, persisting with discipline, and holding to our dreams are the internal characteristics that drive us to rise from the ashes.

Self-motivation and determination coupled with a support system are quite powerful.

Internal locus of control is primary in the foundation of resilience. Do individuals with internal locus of control make better life choices for personal satisfaction and success? Studying and fostering a strong internal locus of control may prove to be the most critical element in helping those at risk become happier and lead healthier and more productive lives. With a strong internal locus of control, we are self-directed and motivated. We look to others for support, but we assume the responsibility for our own choices.

Taking personal responsibility for your life places you on an advanced track. Personal responsibility is crucial in your own life in relationship to self-direction. Do you feel that you can take charge in your life and move forward, or do you feel like a victim with no way out of the trap in which you find yourself?

Feeling that you have the power to make choices and the ability to follow your own path are both results of awakening to your Divine Inner Power. If you feel trapped and unable to move around freely emotionally or physically, use the techniques and processes in this book to support you in awakening to your Divine Inner Power.

Your Support System

Surround yourself with supportive people who help you achieve your dreams and live a more fulfilled life. This support fuels your desire to share your happiness and success with others.

While your internal support is perhaps the most critical component in determining your happiness and success, having a reflection of that strength and vision from those who support you on your path is helpful. Free yourself of those who sap your energy and keep company with those who see your divine light.

The Divine Declaration

The Divine Declaration VI – Support for My Life Growth and Dreams

When in the course of my life, I find repression, unhappiness, ill-health, a chaotic state of mind, and a general sense of hopelessness, it is essential that I release any old programming, ties to the past, current situations, or people who are not supportive of my happiness, my ability to pursue my dreams, my general well-being, and my spiritual, emotional, and mental growth. I now assume my connection to God, the Divine Source, and recognize the power residing inside of me. I was created by the Divine Source; therefore, it must hold true that I am connected to this divinity and have access to a greater power. It is inside of me. It is my divine inheritance. I choose a new path of freedom from the albatross of unworthiness today. The weight is gone. A new world awaits me. And, so it is.

Thank you, Universe. Thank you, God.

Your Support System

I now accept as true and hold these truths to be evident: I will build my support system. My internal support system and my connection with my Divine Inner Power are quite powerful. It is important that I surround myself with people who support me. I release anyone who is hindering my spiritual growth and personal development. To live my dreams, I must look upward toward the open sky and keep my vision ahead. It is no longer necessary to keep the company of people who interfere with this vision. I let go of the naysayers and bless them out of my life. My life is on track with my highest good, and I fill my life with people who support my highest good. I also support them on their journey to live their dreams. We share a mutual trust and encourage happiness, health, and abundance. I find greater support as I connect with my Divine Inner Power. This power is operating in my life always. I know I am a divine spark of God, the Divine Source, and this connection provides me great strength and determination.

This is my Divine Declaration.

Chapter Seven

Love, Gratitude, and Forgiveness

The Divine Declaration

"Love is what we were born with. Fear is what we learned here."
— Marianne Williamson

"Feeling grateful or appreciative of someone or something in your life actually attracts more of the things that you appreciate or value into your life."
— Dr. Christiane Northrup

"Forgive all who have offended you, not for them, but for yourself."
— Harriet Nelson

Love, Gratitude, and Forgiveness

How do we identify love and what it means to us? Love carries different meanings and experiences, and may bring forth feelings of both happiness and sadness. Love is not necessarily in degrees but is multi-faceted and multi-dimensional. You may love your lover intensely, and also love your companion animals, children, parents, family, and friends with equal intensity, but experientially different from who you love romantically. While we love our romantic partner with romantic love, we love our family with a familial love that encompasses dimensions equally deep and abiding. You may love humanity with agape love, but you do not necessarily want to share your time with all of these people individually or intimately. You also may attach the word *love* to how you feel about the earth, the things you do or even to the foods that you eat. Love includes a variety of things and encompasses different aspects of our life.

Because love is a fundamental and vast part of our experience, shouldn't we begin with loving our *Self*? How can we really love another if we do not love our *Self*? The *Self* to which I am referring is written with a capital S and is your divine *Self*, who you really are, not the ego or superficial arrogance and self-obsession rooted in insecurity. Loving your divine *Self* includes understanding your desires, being patient and non-judgmental of your *Self*, and living in acceptance of your perceived flaws and admirable qualities. It is your *Self* that seeks the higher good for you and for all. It is the REAL you that recognizes divinity and is connected to your Divine Inner Power. If someone asks us for a basket of wheat, can we give them the wheat if we have none in our own basket? No. <u>Nor can we really give love if we do not love ourselves.</u>

Many people confuse needing someone with loving that person. Need is possessive, obsessive, and controlling, and it burdens a relationship with <u>many negative expectations</u>. A person in need of a relationship may merely want to be with someone. They may need financial security or a mate to satisfy a societal role. Often having a romantic partner makes him or her feel worthy. People operating from need expect someone else to bring them happiness or take care of their needs. Therefore, especially in romantic relationships, much of the time people are experiencing need or working out some emotional baggage instead of experiencing a healthy loving relationship.

People enter into relationships for various reasons, including the need to work out their emotional relationship with a parental figure. A woman may find herself involved with a man who is unable to commit emotionally or who keeps her at arm's length. A man may choose to marry a woman who is a damsel in distress or a woman who is cool, aloof, or emotionally disengaged. If these people look closely at the dynamics of the relationship, they will likely find some of the same dynamics in their relationship with their mothers or fathers. The woman with the emotionally distant man seeks her father's love through her significant other. The man with the damsel in distress seeks control of his emotions related to his mother. They attempt to resolve their parental relationships through romantic connections that represent unfulfilled childhood needs. Although not necessarily a conscious choice, this scenario plays out nonetheless. The partner cannot fill the void or supply the insatiable need.

Healthy relationships based on love, instead of need, are rooted in emotionally healthy individuals who love themselves and understand their value as an individual before engaging in a relationship with another person. Emotionally healthy individuals know that their happiness and power in life resides within them. They have recognized and hold their own sense of value and do not seek a relationship as a means of personal validation.

In *Atlas Shrugged*, Ayn Rand shares this relationship framework profoundly through one of her characters —

> But, in fact, a man's sexual choice is the result and the sum of his fundamental convictions. Tell me what a man finds sexually attractive and I will tell you his entire philosophy of life. Show me the woman he sleeps with and I will tell you his valuation of himself.

In my relationship with my ex-husband, I confused need with love. I felt an emotional connection because he was adopted and I grew up in foster homes. For his own reasons, he couldn't extend himself beyond his own wants and needs, but I thought if I loved him enough, I could persuade him to live up to his potential. In turn, he would love me for rescuing him. At the time, I had no idea of what I was really engaging in emotionally, I just knew that I would try to make the marriage work, but I learned that I couldn't make it work alone. I worked very hard and pressured him to conform to my idea of a romantic relationship. He resisted.

I intently began my inner search when we divorced. Later, I realized I had subconsciously thought if I could save him, maybe I could also save myself from the pain of my childhood. If I could get this emotionally benign man to respond, I could overcome the loss of my natural father's love. I didn't realize why I worked so hard to maintain a relationship that wasn't right for me until I saw a counselor during the separation. Through the counseling sessions, I realized that I had mistaken need for love. I needed to save someone, and through this process, save myself. I thought I needed a man's love at whatever costs. Then I could subconsciously say, "Ah, the wound of my absent father is healed."

I worked on my inner awareness after my divorce and realized that I didn't respect, trust, or love my ex-husband. This understanding was quite a revelation considering the work and diligence I had exerted in the relationship. Eventually, I worked through my attraction to men who are unable to connect emotionally and my need to make them someone other than who they are. I have since developed discernment and learned to love my *Self*. Through this awareness, I find I am now attracted to men who are capable of a healthy emotional connection.

By observing my past relationships and others' relationships, I believe this lack of *Self* love is at the center of many unhappy relationships. When you pursue the inner path and truly love your *Self*, you are then able to love another. Until you love your *Self*, a relationship is a labor of working through very heavy emotional baggage.

Yes, the divorce rate is high, but many people also stay in marriages and continue to work out their emotional baggage on their partner. Just because a relationship is long-term doesn't necessarily mean it is a happy one. Two people may stay together because they feel they are matched at the level of their emotional needs. A mature, healthy relationship is a connection between two people who are not caught in the black hole of need. Instead, they fulfill their own life desires and dreams. Their relationship is the icing on the cake — it is not the cake. Getting in touch with who we are is the forerunner to attracting a healthy relationship.

Someone once commented on a famous person's violent relationship with his wife. "He must have really loved her," this person said. This man had stalked and beaten his wife; eventually, she died a violent death. The woman speaking to me equated obsession with love. She deduced that if he wanted to be with her that badly, he must have really loved her. What she thought was love is actually control and obsession — not at all the real thing.

This kind of baggage is too heavy to carry in a relationship and can be deadly. Understanding the difference between love and respect and control and dependence is important. Through understanding the nature of love, we eschew co-dependent or controlling relationships and move forward to relationships of greater harmony and balance.

Love is complex and has many faces. The most important place to begin is to get in touch with your lovability. We are powerful when we love *ourSelves* and our divine source to which we are connected. From this position of internal power, we are able to extend this love to others.

My brother once commented, "Love has a way of showing itself." How true. Giving and receiving love requires us to know our own value. With our value in place, we can accept love and share the jewel inside of us.

Loving yourself comes naturally as you get in touch with your Divine Inner Power. You'll find it is easy to share what you have in abundance. Start by loving yourself, and instinctively you will share your love with the world.

GRATITUDE

Gratitude is a beautiful and necessary part of life. Living with an attitude of gratitude is a wonderful and expansive feeling. Think of a time when you were thankful for something, even if it seemed insignificant. I can think of numerous things for which I am grateful, and these things bring a smile. If you haven't thought of anything yet, let's look at a few things to get you started.

While reading this book, you are able to see and comprehend. Can you hear, walk, talk, laugh, cry, and smile? Do you enjoy nature, your children, family, friends, and are you able to eat and enjoy your favorite food? Let this list stimulate your gratitude. I'm sure you can think of many other things for which you are thankful.

When we accept and believe in the concept "what we focus on we create more of," we can understand how gratitude is a substantial piece of connecting with our Divine Inner Power. If we focus on the wonderful things in our lives that bring us joy and free our souls to soar, universal law creates more of these experiences.

For instance, thinking of how you moved through challenging times creates more strength for the next challenge you face. When we focus on successful, happy relationships or experiences in our life, we create energy around and within us to attract more of this energy. Gratitude, what a beautiful thing. The more I focus on how excited I am about writing, the more freely the words flow.

Thanksgiving, a special day of gratitude, is my favorite holiday. I enjoy the day to celebrate a plentiful harvest. The whole event — the beautiful autumn leaves, the colors of the food being harvested, the mood of the day — stirs excitement in my soul. The cornucopia is a great symbol for Thanksgiving! A horn-of-plenty, overflowing with a bountiful harvest, is a great visualization for abundance. As you work on your gratitude, draw a cornucopia and write your words of gratitude or draw and cut and paste what you would like to see overflowing in your life.

Every day is a day of Thanksgiving as we live in concert with our divinity and use our personal power to create our life cornucopia filled with what we want to experience. Another way to recognize and connect with your gratitude is to create a gratitude journal. Every day, record a journal entry of at least one thing you are thankful for during that day. Did someone say a kind word to you? Did you get to pet your precious dog or cat today? Relate to someone you love? Read a good book? Enjoy the sun or the rain, sunrise or sunset? Have a great hair day? Have a bad hair day and not care?

The Divine Declaration

Consider all of the wonderful things in your life. It is amazing how your world will open up and how you feel joy and marvel at the wonders in your world. Survey your own life and make a note of everything for which you are grateful — from the great and wondrous to the small gems scattered throughout your everyday experience. You may find a smile and create more of the energy to manifest what you desire.

What does this gratitude look like in the physical realm of your life? When you get in touch with your gratitude, you find more to be grateful for. In the face of adversity, when it seems there is little to be thankful for, remembering our divinity is helpful. During a challenging time, we can utilize our Divine Inner Power to bring us back to our greatest *Self*.

Find at least one thing for which you can say, "I am thankful for _____." This is a catalyst to help you generate a whole list of things for which you are grateful. Practicing gratitude helps you maintain your equilibrium in times when you feel emotionally unbalanced.

FORGIVENESS

What about forgiveness? Can you hear the haunting organ music when forgiveness is mentioned? Where do we begin?

Forgiveness elicits a wrinkled brow and a sinking feeling in many of us. How can we possibly forgive someone who has wronged us?

If we forgive, do we have to rekindle a relationship with someone from the past? Does this person deserve our charity? Furthermore, if we do forgive those who have wronged us, how can we honestly feel a release from the anger, hurt, disappointment, grief, wound to our self-value, animosity, teeth-grinding and jaw-clenching rage that we hold inside? Can we truly let go of the grudge?

Is it possible to be able to forgive and forget? Even if we should forgive, why would we want to?

To begin this process, let's review how Jesus dealt with forgiveness. In the midst of his crucifixion, he said, "Father forgive them; for they know not what they do."

We might look at circumstances in our own lives and yield to this understanding. People who are malicious, untrustworthy, emotionally disconnected, or incapable of caring actually "know not what they do." This recognition does not excuse the person, but it helps us to release our inner struggle with the notion that this individual could have done something different. The person was not spiritually or emotionally evolved enough to handle it differently. This knowing, at the soul level, is where we release the bondage and pain of our injuries.

Why is it important for us to forgive, and how is it advantageous to our well-being? When you think of someone who has hurt you, you can feel muscles tighten, and you likely feel sad or angry. Is this a feeling and experience that you would like to continue? Probably not. However, you might rationalize, "I can handle these feelings. You don't understand: What they did to me was devastating and unacceptable. Forgive them? Well, I'm not sure I'm ready or that they deserve my forgiveness."

I can think of several people, including my biological mother, one of my foster parents, an ex-husband, and a few previous co-workers whom I have found challenging to forgive. I had to work through the disappointment, sadness, and anger involved with each situation. While I could intellectualize why they did what they did, exploring my painful emotions was not an easy task.

For the early part of my life, I had repressed and turned inward the anger and disappointment of being given up to foster care and living with a foster parent who treated me with indifference. Through my inner work, I discovered that these emotions were causing my sore jaw muscles, neck pain, and malfunctioning digestive system. I literally shut down internally. The suppressed anger and inability as a child to express my feelings manifested through a clenched jaw, tightened neck and shoulder muscles, and intestinal spasms. This constriction was the result of many years of internalized painful emotions.

FORGIVENESS PROCESSES

A great exercise to work through forgiveness is to write a letter to the people you feel have hurt you. In this letter, let them know what they did to hurt you, why it hurt you, and how disappointed or angry you are due to the transgression. Once you are in touch with the pain, you might ask why they did what they did to you and how they would respond now to your pain. The writing of this letter allows you to gain insight and perspective, whether the infraction was intentional or unintentional.

You do not mail the letter to the person. It is a tool to assist you in releasing your pain and beginning to forgive. You may gain understanding that people, sometimes, are not evolved emotionally and may have been doing their best at the time. While their behavior is not acceptable, this bit of information may help you free the weight that is keeping you down and sinking in your pain.

To forgive does not mean you have to become friends with the person who hurt you. Instead, forgiveness can be the agent that frees you to move on and lighten your energy. Many spiritual teachers point out that we form a strong bond to the people we feel injured us. This bond holds us captive until we forgive — only forgiveness cuts the binding tie.

After you've written the letter to your transgressor, reply to yourself with a letter from that person. This is your chance for them to say to you, "I'm sorry for hurting you," and perhaps to salve your wound. During this part of the healing, the sting will lessen. Would you like for the person to say, "I was wrong to treat you this way," for example? If so, write this response. Do not suppress your emotions when writing this letter. This is a great opportunity for you to allow a sigh of real relief in the forgiveness process.

Through using the letter writing process and the following techniques to release pain surrounding hurtful events, I have found forgiveness for the people I felt had wronged me in some way.

Another effective forgiveness process is to imagine a gold frame surrounding the face of anyone with whom you would like to forgive. See them inside the frame and visualize the frame and their image transforming to gold dust. Blow the gold dust out into the universe and watch it dissipate into the air and trickle out into space. This beautiful exercise helps you break down the negative energy and transform it for healing.

One additional and interesting forgiveness process is a balloon release image. Place everyone you are ready to forgive in an open

The Divine Declaration

field together and tie a balloon to each one. As you work with forgiving each individual, visualize the person floating up to the sky and out into eternity as your pain and grief float away with each person you release.

One final forgiveness process is through channeling the anger, pain, and frustration into Mother Earth and experiencing a transformation of energy. This process was also covered in Chapter Five. See the negative energy as an orange light traveling through your body, through the spine and chakras, then down and out of the bottoms of your feet into the earth. Observe the energy as it transforms into a rainbow of light energy, lifting from the earth and expanding out into the universe.

Try variations of this process and the visualizations. Sometimes I allow this rainbow of light to travel up and around my body, and reenter through the crown chakra on the top of my head and then leave my body through the heart chakra in small, heart-shaped rainbows or solid pastel hearts, sending love and light out to the world.

Continue working with these processes until thinking of the person who hurt you no longer stings or causes tension. When you reach a point of forgiveness, you feel detached and indifferent in relationship to the event or person connected to the internal strife you formerly experienced. This detachment may come and go at first, until you finally forgive and no longer feel pain when you think of the event or individual.

Make this a pleasant — not dreaded — process. Forgiveness is

Love, Gratitude, and Forgiveness

freeing for your inner well-being and a primary component of re-establishing your personal power.

Love, gratitude, and forgiveness are foundational stepping stones on your journey of personal enlightenment and power. Loving yourself, finding gratitude in everyday things, and forgiving someone for the pain they may have caused you promotes a healthy sense of *Self*. These aspects of your life are building blocks connecting you with your Divine Inner Power.

The Divine Declaration

The Divine Declaration VII – Love, Gratitude, and Forgiveness

When in the course of my life, I find repression, unhappiness, ill-health, a chaotic state of mind, and a general sense of hopelessness, it is essential that I release any old programming, ties to the past, current situations, or people who are not supportive of my happiness, my ability to pursue my dreams, my general well-being, and my spiritual, emotional, and mental growth. I now assume my connection to God, the Divine Source, and recognize the power residing inside of me. I was created by the Divine Source; therefore, it must hold true that I am connected to this divinity and have access to a greater power. It is inside of me. It is my divine inheritance. I choose a new path of freedom from the albatross of unworthiness today. The weight is gone. A new world awaits me. And, so it is.

Thank you, Universe. Thank you, God.

Love, Gratitude, and Forgiveness

I now accept as true and hold these truths to be evident: I now understand that I must love my *Self* in order to really be capable of loving another. It is through understanding I am a spark of the Divine Source that I am able to tap into my Divine Inner Power and learn to love me. I am love, loving, loved, and lovable. I am grateful that I now know these valuable truths about my *Self*. I spend time each day remembering my value. If I am in touch with my divinity, I see the divinity in others. I start each day with gratitude. I find at least one thing for which I am grateful every day. My gratitude expands and opens my life to more wonderful things daily. I can forgive others who may have hurt me along the way. It is for me that I work on forgiveness. I now know that when I forgive someone, I free myself from the bondage of pain. I release my *Self* from this pain. It is clear that loving me, focusing on things for which I am grateful, and forgiving past hurts releases me to live the divine life I deserve.

This is my Divine Declaration.

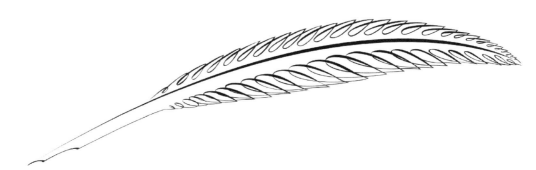

Section Four

Live in Connection With Your Divine Inner Power

Chapter Eight

Your Divine Right Livelihood

The Divine Declaration

"I have learned, that if one advances confidently in the direction of his dreams, and endeavors to live the life he has imagined, he will meet with a success unexpected in common hours."

— Henry David Thoreau

Your Divine Right Livelihood

What's your passion? Have you decided what you would really like to do in life? What is your life purpose or divine right livelihood? At some time in your life you have probably questioned what you would like to do for a career. You may have taken one avenue and then changed direction, or you may be just beginning your journey on the path of your divine right livelihood. It is also possible that you have known your life purpose since childhood. However, for some of us, narrowing this search can take time, clear focus, and persistence. It is a great part of our life and certainly deserves our attention.

Knowing our life purpose generates positive energy with which we connect. When we are in our purpose, our inner power drives us, and we thrive on the energy it produces. To discover your right livelihood you can connect with natural talents and interests through self-assessment tests, or you may benefit from reading material addressing this specific aspect of your life. Visualize your ideal livelihood and journal the process to clarify your purpose. Write your desires and goals in an affirmative tone to gain clarity and define your direction.

The Divine Declaration

Help people emotionally, spiritually, or physically. Dig in the dirt and grow plants that either beautify your environment or place food on your table. Prepare food or build homes. Enter the hustle-bustle of the corporate ranks or tackle the complexity of engineering, physics, or astronomy. Where would we be without those who study the wonders of nature and provide us with music and art? Your ultimate purpose could lead you anywhere.

To get in touch with your right livelihood, again, connect with your inner power. Listen to your inner guidance — the divine voice within you.

Write the following questions and your answers. Do not be modest or reluctant with your answers; let the real you come through to get in touch.

1. *If I had all of the money I could use, what would I do with my time, or if no one was prompting me to do otherwise, what would I like to do with my life?*
2. *What does my ideal life look and feel like to me? Be specific. Include your life's purpose, relationships, home, and lifestyle. Tap into what how this life feels to you.*
3. *What are my interests?*
4. *What talents do I have to offer?*
5. *What am I willing to do to create my ideal life?*
6. *What are my primary belief systems about who I am?*
7. *Who do I admire, and why?*
8. *Am I willing to live my truth?*
9. *When I think of spending time doing this_____, I feel exhilarated or in the now moment.*

10. *Why do I want to spend my time in this way?*
11. *Do I want to work in an office environment or from home?*
12. *What are some steps I can take to begin to live my divine right livelihood?*

Calm your mind and allow your inner voice to speak to you. Review your answers. You may want to explore your divine right livelihood space daily in order to really feel and connect with your ideal life direction. Feeling excitement or pleasure increases this energy for you and again, because like attracts like, revel in this energy. Take your time and pay attention to what your innate talent is shouting at you.

Finding your life purpose is an adventure and is instrumental in reaching your fulfillment. If I had listened to my intuition earlier in the process of finding my divine right livelihood, I could have saved myself some time and energy. However, the process and experience was interesting, and I learned what I would like to do with my life.

Getting in touch with your life purpose may include some interesting research. Career assessment tests are helpful in order to gain insight into your likes, dislikes, and areas of competency. I have taken the Meyers-Briggs and the MAPP tests in my career search. Both produced considerably accurate results.

Books can help direct you to your life's purpose. I found *Do What You Love the Money Will Follow* by Marsha Sinetar and *What Color is Your Parachute* by Richard Bolles helpful in my pursuit. *Follow Your Bliss*, by Hal Zina Bennett and Susan T. Sparrow, is an excellent read. Caroline Myss' book, *Sacred Contracts, Awakening Your Divine Potential,* may also prove helpful.

I devoted much time during my collegiate years searching for my divine purpose. At different points, I wanted a career in aeronautics, forestry, botany, cosmetology, and psychology, just to name a few. It was quite puzzling to have so many interests and not be sure what I would do with my life. It was actually a family joke. If they didn't know where to find me during that time in my life, they would jokingly say, "Oh, she must be at the career center."

I was diligent in my search and found that being an astronaut was out — I should have started training as a youngster. A forest ranger was too similar to a police officer in the woods, so I decided to keep hiking as a hobby, not a career. There was much more to being a botanist than just traipsing though the jungles like I envisioned through watching National Geographic films. I wasn't sure at the time how I could possibly finance a Ph.D. in psychology. Cutting and styling hair was fun and creative, but not as a full-time career. So I thought, maybe an aerospace engineer — I do love the space program.

Moving forward with this decision, I met with a professor at the Georgia Institute of Technology School of Aerospace Engineering and I began the track at school to become a rocket scientist. It seemed an interesting, admirable, and challenging career. I prepared by taking higher level math courses, which was not my best subject.

During this time, I was also writing papers for English and Psychology classes, receiving As, and enduring the embarrassment of being asked to read my papers in class. Because I was going to be a rocket scientist, I didn't give the psychology and writing too much thought at the time. I had to focus on working hard in trigonometry and getting through calculus. Interestingly, I had an awakening my first day of calculus. When the professor started the lecture, I realized clearly this was not where I belonged. Without hesitation, I left the class with a definitive understanding. I knew I wasn't going to be a rocket scientist. It was somewhat disheartening, but at the same time I felt a great sense of relief. I recognized that my talents just weren't in engineering. I still loved the space program, but I realized writing and psychology seemed a natural fit for me.

I was just beginning my spiritual journey and perhaps I could help others like the authors of the books I was devouring had helped me along my path. Finally, I had it! It wasn't a struggle, and I was totally interested in the journey. I was receiving affirmations. Again, the research papers I wrote for class were used as examples. Now I was paying attention, what a concept! I received my undergraduate degree in psychology. I worked on my writing skills through creative writing classes, wrote short stories and articles for two company newsletters, copy for direct marketing campaigns, and published articles in an industry newspaper and several spiritual newsletters. How fun, to love the journey and not struggle so hard with the process. I was finally in tune with my purpose, not fighting to gain a foothold in something that wasn't the natural flow.

A seasoned writer spoke at a luncheon I recently attended. He shared his story of coming into his writing career. As a youngster he was infatuated with baseball and wanted to become a major league baseball player. He signed up with the minor league, but his baseball career abruptly ended soon after it began. Disheartened, the young man decided to pursue an engineering degree. He told us that he wasn't even sure at the time the function of an engineer. In spite of his uncertainty, he enrolled as an engineering major, but he also signed up for a writing class. At the end of the year, the writing professor pulled him aside and told him he thought he had talent and maybe should consider journalism as a career. A new writing career was born. He became a sports columnist and now writes books for his livelihood.

Stories abound of people determined to overcome the odds or the naysayers. Apple Computer and Federal Express are two great examples of companies founded by entrepreneurs who listened to their own counsel and eschewed the naysayers. These men were told their ideas simply weren't possible, but they didn't take *no* for an answer. You know the rest of the story. It is wise to listen to others who are successful or who have your interest at heart, yet it is equally wise to listen to your own intuitive counsel.

Another interesting example of someone who had the courage and tenacity to pursue her dream is NASA's first African American female astronaut, Mae Jemison. She had to rise above naysayers projecting their views of what her life should look like. Instead she chose her own path. In her kindergarten class, the teacher asked the children one by one what they wanted for a career when they grew up. Jemison wanted to be a scientist. Her teacher immediately corrected her: she should become a nurse. Jemison knew the teacher was trying to steer her to a more realistic career in a time when not only a woman, but certainly not a black woman, could become a scientist. However, Jemison decided not to limit herself because of others' limited imagination.

To discover your strengths, talents, and what resonates with you requires some inner work. Following the status quo into jobs that make it difficult to go to work is not living in our highest potential. It is draining and promotes an unhappy life. You can choose your life path as Robert Frost famously spoke of in his poem, "The Road Not Taken." The writer decided for himself which road to take. He took the road less traveled, and for him it made all the difference.

Major life decisions such as your Divine Right Livelihood can be challenging. Following your heart or your bliss, instead of succumbing to what others are doing, or expect you to do, requires you to take a brave step. Making your own way and deciding your own path takes courage and determination.

Others may feel threatened by your individuality or your power and tell you, "You can't do that. It simply isn't feasible."

They may inadvertently dampen your dreams by advising you to follow the path of least resistance or to stay with the status quo. For instance, a friend of mine wanted to pursue a career in music, but his father would only pay for college if he sought a business degree.

Change is always an option, even if you decided early on to "do as you were told" for a career path, or you just weren't clear of your direction. Many people have changed directions later in life. I know people who have exited the corporate world in their forties or fifties and struck out to own and manage a bed and breakfast. I also know two women who left careers in nursing. Now one owns her own skin care center, and the other owns a spa. I can think of other people I

The Divine Declaration

know who own their own consulting business rather than working for someone else.

Another one of my friends had several disappointing experiences working for others. Subsequently, she started a business with someone, but her partner left her owing the bills. She steadfastly has paid the bills and now owns a publishing consulting business. Her energy is enthusiastic and positive and continually attracts new business contacts. It is likely that you know people who have decided to follow their hearts to a successful and joyful destination.

Take a moment to identify your greatest desire for your right livelihood. Don't judge. Be open to all possibilities. As soon as you identify your right livelihood path, take one step at a time. Take music lessons, write a book part time, go to evening classes, research your interests, read about others who have succeeded in your area of interest — just take that step and see where it leads you. You don't need to sabotage yourself or your finances in the process. Begin with where you are and propel your energy into following your bliss. You may be amazed at the confirmations you receive on the way.

Look inside at your power and determine what you are seeking for your life. Your life purpose can take form in ways that may be inconceivable to you now. The momentum begins when you take a step in the direction of your dreams. Like a snowball gathering snow on a fast decline, you garner support for your dreams as you engage in your life purpose. Your enthusiasm and dedication affect those around you. Again, like attracts like, and the people with whom you interact during this journey will reflect your dreams. They will be excited for you and help you achieve your goals. You will recognize the "knowing that you know that you know" inner confirmation as you continue along your path.

Some effort on your part is required to recognize your talents and pursue your dreams, but it is a course that makes the difference. When you decide your dream livelihood and path, take a step on that path, and tap into your Divine Inner Power. You are well on your way to your fulfillment. Use the treasure mapping and journaling techniques included in this book to assist you in your endeavor. They are very effective tools for this aspect of your life. You get to decide the direction for your life. If you've waited until later in life to take this step, or if you are just beginning your path, you have the opportunity to succeed. All the best to you!

The Divine Declaration VIII – Discovering and Pursuing My Divine Right Livelihood

When in the course of my life, I find repression, unhappiness, ill-health, a chaotic state of mind, and a general sense of hopelessness, it is essential that I release any old programming, ties to the past, current situations, or people who are not supportive of my happiness, my ability to pursue my dreams, my general well-being, and my spiritual, emotional, and mental growth. I now assume my connection to God, the Divine Source, and recognize the power residing inside of me. I was created by the Divine Source; therefore, it must hold true that I am connected to this divinity and have access to a greater power. It is inside of me. It is my divine inheritance. I choose a new path of freedom from the albatross of unworthiness today. The weight is gone. A new world awaits me. And, so it is.

Thank you, Universe. Thank you, God.

Your Divine Right Livelihood

I now accept as true and hold these truths to be evident: I have decided to pursue my dreams. I take this step forward. I see others who are successful and know that I can be successful, too. I know many people live their dreams and knowing this reinforces my belief in my own ability. I have people in my life who support me on my divine right livelihood path. It is with determination and energy I move forward to live the life I deserve, a life of joy, abundance, and love. I am aligned with my life purpose and find direction with every step I take. I am excited and see myself as successful and fulfilling my purpose daily. My divine right livelihood is a great part of my journey, and I know I have every opportunity to succeed. Love lights the way, joy greets me on my path, and harmony and abundance manifest in all areas of my life. I have hope and faith in my journey now. I find greater confidence and fortitude as I handle each challenge with ease and grace. I share the joy of others as they also pursue their dreams.

This is my Divine Declaration.

Chapter Nine

Opening to the Flow of the Universe and Sharing

The Divine Declaration

"You are either allowing something into your life, or you are rejecting something from entering your life. 'What am I giving access to?' That is the first question to ask yourself. Since life cannot rob from you or take from you without your cooperation, looking at what you are letting in is the place to put your focus."

— Ralph Carpio

"Life is a gift, and it offers us the privilege, opportunity, and responsibility to give something back by becoming more."

— Anthony Robbins

Opening to the Flow of the Universe and Sharing

Open the door to the flow of life. Abandon beating your head against the proverbial brick wall and discover the expansive world awaiting you. Can you think of a time when you said to yourself, "This is too difficult. I am struggling at every turn, and I don't seem to get anywhere. I am going in circles, and my head aches from the internal battle." I can relate. In previous years, I have bloodied my share of bricks on the wall of resistance. However, I have learned the value of relaxing and allowing, rather than battling and whipping my life into shape. Allowing is a more peaceful and effective way of approaching life. I accomplish more with this approach because I'm more attentive and seek to recognize opportunities, instead of hammering my head against the wall of what isn't working in my life.

Allowing divine energy and light to flow into your life gives rise to a remarkable experience. Open the door to the power of the universe and become a vessel for the flow of divine energy. Allow it to flow through you by incorporating methods with which you are comfortable for your growth, such as: meditation, energy healings, reading the writings of masters, or writing your own truths. You may also feel the divine flow as you enjoy nature, your family and friends, or any endeavor in which you experience the "now" moment. Happiness, health, love, and peace are benefits of allowing the universal energy into your consciousness.

OPENING TO THE DIVINE LIFE FLOW

Choose a level of vibration that allows you to open to your highest good. Work to stay in the positive vibration in order to release negative energy. Allow new, refreshing energy to work in your life. As you awaken each morning, know that divine love is with you always and this love surrounds you. It permeates every cell of your physical body and lives in your spirit. This powerful love is a stream of light supporting you throughout your day. Allow this eternal love and light to help you on your path. Remind yourself throughout the day, "I am in the flow of my life. All is well, and everything is in divine order." After you set your intention for a higher level of existence, the journey follows. You recognize signposts along the way, feel that you are in alignment with your purpose, and at times experience intuitive knowing. When we trust in the Universal Divine Law that we are supported by divine love, we find we are happier, more peaceful, positioned to attract our highest good, and better able to reach out to others.

Meditating or simply sitting quietly in nature is an excellent pathway through which to allow the universal flow of energy to

Opening to the Flow of the Universe and Sharing

enter and permeate your whole being with divine light. Imagine a light flowing into your crown chakra and illuminating all of your cells as the light filters through your body and into the earth. Release a stream of light through your heart chakra and allow this energy to return to the universe as a rainbow of light or as hearts of energy sending love into the universe. Perhaps you may choose to release signs of peace such as white doves. Visualize these hearts or signs of peace reaching around the world. This exercise leaves you feeling peaceful, uplifted, and relaxed. *[margin note: Go-chi]*

Flowing with the current is an easier and a less stressful way to live than struggling upstream, kicking and screaming against the flow while getting banged and bruised on rocks of resistance, collecting debris that hinders our growth. Allowing the ebb and flow of life keeps us above the surface where we can easily breathe and relax in the support of our divine power. We can rest in this power knowing that we are eternal and spiritual beings experiencing this human environment in the space and time dimension. Knowing our Divine Inner Power and understanding who we really are brings us great peace. Practice letting life flow through you instead of resisting every change. "Allowing" takes time to embrace, but it is worthwhile. You will observe events and changes happening with synchronicity.

Connect with a greater power and realize there actually is order in the universe. Allow your life to unfold. Keep up your positive attitude and follow the direction of your dreams. Divine love is here to support you.

Connecting with our deep desire releases our power to create

The Divine Declaration

our life dreams. This process doesn't mean you force a relationship into being or take from others. Instead you find what is right for your life, your divine highest good, and allow it to manifest. For example, if you are involved in a relationship that isn't working for you or is not in alignment with your highest good, you receive signals that this relationship is not in sync with your value system, but perhaps you move into denial. Reluctantly, you accept the task of making this situation work, or you try to change the other person. If you are in this situation, step back for a moment and ask yourself, "Is this in my highest good, or am I accepting less than I really want in my life?" This is the question to ask about any situation in your life with which you may be struggling. This question-and-answer process hones your decisions and discernment.

As soon as we understand what we are manifesting and are willing to accept into our life, we are in a wonderful place to allow divinity to flow through us, and to reach out to others who seek greater awareness on their journey. Sharing our truth reinforces our own awareness as we connect with those who resonate with the message. Others echo our message or share with us a unique message that strikes a chord within us. Sharing our truth with others may help them discover their own gem inside. Allowing the information to flow through us, while not being concerned as to who may or may not accept it as part of their truth, is what strengthens us.

Some people have not yet recognized their divinity. Remember

Opening to the Flow of the Universe and Sharing

they will find the light in their own time. We do not need to make sure these people have a brilliant revelation while we watch. Much like the old saying, "When the pupil is ready, the teacher will appear," divine evolution occurs in its own time and manner.

There are many paths to the pinnacle, and each truth leading to the light is important. Some of us learn in a linear way, and some are more circular learners who spiral up to the top. Still others meander along the way, rest and even trek back down the mountain before continuing on the path of enlightenment. These modes of learning are all workable. Each of us is at a different place on our spiritual journey toward the light: the logistics of travel is the variance. The light remains at the top, a steady beacon shining and lighting the way for all who travel.

SHARING YOUR DIVINE OUTFLOW WITH THE UNIVERSE

Beginning with childhood and continuing throughout our lives, sharing is important. It is part of the flow of life. Francois Rabelais, a French monk from the 15th century said, "Nature abhors a vacuum." When we shut down and become totally self-absorbed in an emotional vacuum, we suffocate our divine nature. In contrast, we breathe life into our divine nature through sharing and allowing life to flow. Through allowing and sharing, we process our divine flow and release our truth, compassion, and love to the universe. As we open and allow our light to shine, we live in a space of creative energy. Sharing is the outflow of this tremendous universal energy.

The Divine Declaration

As children, we learn to share toys. As we mature, we share more than toys. We share our lives with family, friends, and others outside our primary circle. Sharing helps teach us personal boundaries and is a part of learning that others exist independently and are not merely extensions of us. It reinforces the notion that they also have their own boundaries. Sharing at a young age teaches generosity and caring about others. It also promotes life-long social skills and the ability to read others' verbal and non-verbal cues.

People who share their life journey, truth, and lessons help many others. For example, motivational and inspirational authors and speakers have helped many people through sharing the lessons they learned and truths they discovered. Og Mandino shared his magnificent story of a time he contemplated the purchase of a gun in a pawn shop window. He was thinking of committing suicide. Instead, he went into the library to warm his weary bones. He was moved to read Napoleon Hill's *Think and Grow Rich*. The book changed his life, and eventually he became a major influence in the inspirational writers' circle. This event in Og Mandino's life is a clear example of Napoleon Hill sharing his truth and how this sharing greatly influenced someone's life.

Consider the people who have shared their stories or talents with the world. We have writers, actors, artists, musicians, doctors, nurses, fire fighters, pastors and chaplains, counselors, teachers, and mentors who have brightened the world with their talents. Our lives are well rounded and enriched with the experiences of others who

Opening to the Flow of the Universe and Sharing

share their lives with us. Think of the people who have shared with you and those whom you admire. These people have probably made your travels a little more interesting and exciting, or made your life challenges more bearable.

I have been significantly affected by the inspiration of other authors' works, through which they have shared their life lessons and messages of hope. Think of someone who has influenced you and helped guide your path. Probably, with little effort, you see the value of sharing. It permeates many aspects of our lives.

I am thankful for the families who shared their homes and love with me. Taking me into their home required work and commitment from all of the family members involved. What a channel to open the flow of the universe, take a child into your home and allow them to become a vital part of your family! I also shared my love with them, but I would venture to guess there were times, especially during my teen years, keeping their commitment must have been trying. However, they didn't just discard me because I wasn't their biological child.

I will always be thankful and remember my friend in high school who often shared her breakfast pastry and lunch with me. When I lived in a home with an indifferent foster parent, our breakfast consisted of oatmeal or a fried egg and the foster children received lunch tickets for a "free lunch." The foster parent wasn't concerned that I was embarrassed by using this ticket and wouldn't give us lunch money, so I opted to not eat lunch. My friend, freely and insistently, shared her food with me. I had accepted not eating lunch, but she has a very generous heart and acted as if it was a natural thing to do. Her generosity had a lasting impact on me. I noticed she was also kind and caring to her family and other friends.

There are many ways we share with others: donating to charities, helping a friend in need, making someone's day brighter, mentoring a child, loving and caring for animals, and supporting others in their dreams. Some people discover their divine right livelihood in sharing and giving or helping others.

Even corporations recognize the importance of sharing information within the corporate structure. Many corporations are promoting "teamwork" in an effort to find solutions to current issues and to encourage new ideas. In her book, *Common Knowledge: How Companies Thrive by Sharing What They Know,* Nancy M. Dixon, explains that the corporate culture may need a noncompetitive internal structure to foster sharing of information. Does the sharing create that cooperative environment? Dixon reveals her findings. "If people begin sharing ideas about issues they see as really important, the sharing itself creates a learning culture." As a side note on her findings, sometimes sharing can be challenging, but even so, remaining open and using discernment with whom you choose to share is one way to remain a channel of light.

If you experience a corporate culture in which management promotes a facade of sharing, it helps to use discernment. In this environment, managers may encourage you to share your ideas and then they either shoot them down in an effort to build up their own ideas or take your idea and claim it as their own when sharing it with

Opening to the Flow of the Universe and Sharing

their superiors. This management style is based in insecurity and fear and suppresses sharing rather than fostering cooperation.

Sharing ideas and remaining open to others in these situations may be difficult. You may think you are asking for insults by allowing yourself to share ideas and being your authentic *Self*. However, on the other edge of the sword is another sharp blade. Not sharing and suppressing your authentic *Self* can be more painful than others refuting your ideas and suggestions. Share your ideas wisely and continue to stay as true to yourself as possible. Perhaps you will choose to eventually move into an environment where you thrive and your ideas are welcomed and rewarded.

Senior citizens have a wealth of information to share. Their knowledge ranges from the wisdom of the ages to insight into what life was like for them as youngsters. I have heard some very interesting stories about farming, childhood games, life during the Great Depression, the fabulous 50s, and how life differed without the conveniences of modern technology. You can look to your own mother or father, grandmother or grandfather, great aunt or uncle to share a part of your history, or you may have a friend who is an elder or wise sage. Sharing with this group is informative, interesting, and one of the most savory items on the menu of life.

When we share with or help others, we create more of that same energy in our life. You may recall times when something in your life just fell into place for you. Recently, I encountered a challenge while I was out of town. I was driving back from a five-hour business

The Divine Declaration

trip and stopped for lunch. I noticed my car's temperature gauge signaling that the engine was overheating. I turned off the engine while I waited for my meal and then promptly drove to the service station across the street. The ladies at the station were most helpful. One lady helped me find a local mechanic, and the other retrieved a water hose to add water to the coolant system. The local mechanic advised me to drive to their location a few miles from the station. The owner was very helpful. He checked the engine and determined he wasn't able to repair it; however, he gave me instructions on how to safely get help if I was stranded in a remote location. He also phoned the local dealership and requested they check it for me. I drove another mile to the dealership and the service manager immediately worked the repair into their schedule. I was on the road to home in just one hour.

During my wait, I chatted with a nice man who was also waiting on repairs. He smiled and told me I helped make his afternoon wait a pleasant experience. I told him that I had enjoyed talking with him as well. I enjoy sharing and helping others, and this situation is just one example of how a circumstance that might have been very taxing worked out, with others helping and sharing with me.

Sharing our truth, time, energy, and love makes the world a brighter place for us all. Allowing the inflow of divine energy and releasing it to the universe creates a brilliant light that illuminates our world. We carry the bright light inside us. As we unfold in our

Opening to the Flow of the Universe and Sharing

divine connection, the darkness shrouding our light is lifted and we shine and bring forth that light for the world to enjoy. Allow the universal flow into your life; share as you awaken to your Divine Inner Power, and illuminate the universe with your internal, eternal bright light.

The Divine Declaration IX — Opening to the Flow of the Universe and Sharing

When in the course of my life, I find repression, unhappiness, ill-health, a chaotic state of mind, and a general sense of hopelessness, it is essential that I release any old programming, ties to the past, current situations, or people that who are not supportive of my happiness, my ability to pursue my dreams, my general well-being, and my spiritual, emotional and mental growth. I now assume my connection to God, the Divine Source, and recognize the power residing inside of me. I was created by the Divine Source; therefore, it must hold true that I am connected to this divinity and have access to a greater power. It is inside of me. It is my divine inheritance. I choose a new path of freedom from the albatross of unworthiness today. The weight is gone. A new world awaits me. And, so it is.

Thank you, Universe. Thank you, God.

Opening to the Flow of the Universe and Sharing

I now accept as true and hold these truths to be evident: I am open to the abundance of the universe. I open my heart, soul, and mind to all the good things that I am attracting into my life. I know that God is infinite and universal supply is abundant and infinite. I allow wonderful adventures, beautiful relationships, a healthy body and mind, and abundant resources and means to fulfill my divine right path in life. I am open to sharing my life with others. Opening to the abundance of the universe is allowance. Sharing is the outflow, creating space for new expansive energy into my life. It is the cycle of universal abundance. I receive, give, and receive again. I create a continual cycle of blessings in my life and in the lives of others through sharing. I release the old and open to the new. With enthusiasm, I allow the power of the universe into my life! Infinite love encircles me and permeates every aspect of my life. Love and light guide my unfolding path day by day. I am more peaceful as I trust divine love. Support accompanies me on my journey every step of the way. I know my highest good is in divine order as well as the highest good of all. I remain true to my authentic *Self* on this journey. I am open and loving. From my internal center of love and light, I send love and light out to the universe.

This is my Divine Declaration.

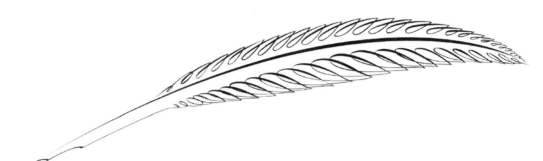

Section Five

Stand Tall and Experience a Life of Divine Inner Power

Chapter Ten

Reinforcement Tools for Connecting With Your Divine Inner Power

The Divine Declaration

"You are never given a wish without being given the power to make it true.
 You may have to work for it, however."
— Richard Bach

Reinforcement Tools: Connecting With Your Divine Inner Power

We attend school with an open mind, ready to allow new information into our realm of thought. The universe is infinite, so why not go to the universe with an open pipeline to allow your divine connection and welcome the flow of wonderful things into your life? This pipeline only requires you to open the valve of acceptance. We open our minds to knowledge in school; we open our mind and heart to our Divine Inner Power.

Awaken your spirit to the knowledge that you can create a beautiful and powerful life. While this journey may require some inner work, it can be great fun, and you will find the reward and adventure far outweighs the due diligence. Awakening to your Divine Inner Power is one of the most important and rewarding things you can do; your life depends on it. This power is the critical component of your success in life. It is your lifeline to joy, abundance, and inner peace. Don't wait any longer to get in touch with your greatest asset.

The world is ready, willing, and able to assist you in your awakening to and connecting with Divine Inner Power. One great way to get started is working with a mentor or teacher. Look around you at the people in your life who can help make a difference for you. You will find one, perhaps several, who will be helpful to you. Counseling or mentoring may involve a teacher, mentor, coach, or professional counselor. It doesn't have to take any certain form. There are several "teachers" who have helped me open to my power — authors, a pastoral and spiritual counselor, several college professors, my foster mother, other family members, friends, a general physician, a psychotherapist/energy healer, a Tai Chi instructor, a chiropractor, and retreat leaders.

Another tool for awakening is to read material developed by others who have successfully pursued a path to their power. Review the books I have recommended in my bibliography and choose one or two to explore, or attend a class, seminar, or retreat that is supportive of you living in your power. Reading books, attending events, retreats, and accessing personal mentors have proved helpful in my quest to unlock and connect with my Divine Inner Power.

READING FOR INSPIRATION

Read books written by others who have embarked on their inner journey. Reading inspirational books helps you connect to your Divine Inner Power and is an effective, fun way to advance you on your path. As the saying goes, "If you want to be successful, ask someone who is already a success." You may seek additional support in your life if you are experiencing challenges in a relationship, your health, finances and career fulfillment, or determining your divine right livelihood path. These are common challenges we all face.

Often it is in the darkest hours when you grow and learn more

Reinforcement Tools: Connecting With Your Divine Inner Power

than you might have imagined. It can be an awakening to read something that stirs your soul in the dark of night, something that inspires you to take the next step on your journey to reach your potential, and live a more joyful and richer life.

I embarked on this inner journey with excitement and fortitude after a friend shared Richard Bach's book *Illusions*. My foster mother was already searching for her own answers and between her support and the book, I eagerly began my journey toward the light.

This was a confusing time in my life. I was in the final stages of a divorce and angry at myself for accepting so little in a relationship. I was disillusioned by my sense of failure.

My mom told me, "Happiness comes from within."

I responded abruptly, "But it is other people who are making me unhappy."

She countered with, "Oh no, you are allowing them to affect you. You may choose to stop their effect at any time. We choose our happiness or unhappiness with every situation. So choose your happiness now regardless of their actions."

Bach's *Illusions* confirmed her advice and catapulted me to a greater understanding. Other authors and their stories have shattered my old trembling belief system and helped to revive my life. Richard Bach, Deepak Chopra, Wayne Dyer, Ralph Waldo Emerson, John Harricharan, Louise Hay, Ernest Holmes, Napoleon Hill, Og Mandino, Dan Millman, Joseph Murphy, Norman Vincent Peale, Sogyal Rinpoche, Baird Spalding, Marianne Williamson, and Hal Zina Bennett are among the authors whose writings have changed my life. There are also many others you may explore in addition to this list. You will find what resonates with you and recognize your truth with an affirming "Ah, ha! I get this, it is powerful information. I will take this information and utilize it."

Some provide you great insight; others teach you ways to change your day-to-day life; and others offer an entertaining story with a message that empowers you. Take what resonates with you and leave the rest. Reading about someone's life and the challenges he or she faced or the great revelations this person experienced helps to direct us on our path and maintain our focus. Please see the list of books in Recommended Reading at the end of this book for additional reading that provided light on my path.

CLASSES AND SEMINARS

Spirituality classes, seminars, and expos can also help guide you on the path of discovery. Attending any of these yields opportunities to be with like minds. You will meet other people who share your life's direction, glean some insight from the life journey of others, participate in experiential exercises with others, share with a support group, or gain from classroom instruction.

In the beginning of my spiritual journey, I stepped out of my everyday life to attend a week-long spiritual retreat in Colorado. I was voraciously reading spiritual and self-help books, and decided I wanted to reach out to others. I discovered a retreat listed in a spiritual publication and thought it could be fun to attend. I had always wanted to visit Colorado, so this trip would be a two-pronged experience — a spiritual and travel adventure. I was a little overwhelmed at first, but the retreat turned out to be interesting, fun, and enlight-

Reinforcement Tools: Connecting With Your Divine Inner Power

ening. The leaders, whose spiritual pseudonyms were Angel and Ascension, were seasoned in prayer and meditation. The food was prepared by an excellent chef we called Sage. We enjoyed vegetarian meals, private meditation in the Rockies, and prayer with the retreat leaders. While some of the retreat was a little overwhelming for me as a novice, I was able to get in touch with my gratitude and experience a deep compassion for some of the attendees. During this retreat, the leaders introduced me to the spiritually powerful *A Course in Miracles*. I practiced the course every day for a year as recommended and continue to refer to these beautiful teachings.

One year after the retreat in Colorado, I left my accounting job, suspended my college education, and traveled from Georgia to Maine to live for the summer. I had great hopes of finding a new perspective for my life. I located a bed and breakfast inn on the coast and was hired to help in the garden, serve food, assist the chef, clean rooms, and work in the goat barn. The innkeepers raised Nubian goats and made award-winning goat cheese at the inn. It was a wondrous summer. Friends from Georgia kept their sailboat in Maine, and I was afforded the incredible opportunity to sail with them. After dining at the inn one evening, we set out to sail for a few days. My friends were very generous and capable sailors and it was this voyage that ignited my love of sailing. I enjoyed their company, meals prepared by a fabulous cook, and an exciting adventure led by a super captain. Remembering my time with them brings warmth and a smile.

This adventure was an effort to get away from it all. I remember my mother's sad good-bye when I left for Maine. We were both sad, but I knew I had to go and see for myself if changing locations made

The Divine Declaration

a difference in my life. I learned that changing locations did not change me. I took my problems with me to Maine, and when I returned I still needed to work through them. As Ralph Waldo Emerson wisely stated, "Though we travel the world over to find the beautiful, we must carry it with us or we find it not." When I returned, I continued working fervently on my spirituality and personal development.

During my years of inner study, I have enjoyed time alone in the mountains hiking and absorbing the magnificence of nature, earned a degree in psychology, learned to play the guitar, completed a basic sailing ground school course, taken time for personal prayer and meditation, gained great personal insight through counseling, experienced energy healing through working with a psychotherapist/healer, taken classes in Tai Chi, and attended spiritual seminars in my search for inspiration and my Divine Inner Power. These bright spots on my journey have provided nuggets of my divine awareness along the way.

Connecting to my Divine Inner Power has been a fun and interesting mission and is now a way of life for me. However, there have been times when I have struggled with the status quo. The further I go and the higher I climb, the more difficult it is to be with others who are not interested in pursuing their inner growth, are living in a mask, and not being their authentic selves. Being around people bragging about how much money they make, the size or location of their home, their possessions, job status, or who they know is a deafening sound. It is a constant reminder of Jonathan, in *Jonathan Livingston Seagull*, as he leaves the flock to pursue his dreams of flight. He could not understand the flock's plight, how they could participate in just merely existing, of feverishly squawking and fighting for food while the fishermen toss them scraps. Why didn't they want more for their lives? The competition and lack of integrity to "get ahead" is like watching the gulls fighting at the landfill for garbage. Jonathan sought a higher path.

While the road less traveled or flying higher isn't always the easy path, it is the worthwhile one. What do we have in our lives if we never connect with our Divine Inner Power and live only for impressing others and transitory things? A nice home and nice surroundings is certainly a plus in life, but they must be attained through manifestation of our belief in abundance, inner worth, and divine power, not from a process of collecting items to impress others or fill a personal void. Many times those who simply focus on the outer will do almost anything to get what it is they want. Stealing, lying, cheating, pretending, and living behind a mask, are avenues people may travel as they squawk and peck for the scraps. Manifesting the life we want from a space of divine awareness does not require or even invoke a lifestyle of unethical actions. Authentic living and courage are main ingredients in the foundation for manifesting a life of your choosing. Connecting to your divinity opens this space of authenticity and courage.

COUNSELING OR COACHING

Working with a counselor, teacher, or mentor is another effective way to process old negative emotions, shift your thoughts, and connect with your Divine Inner Power. Again, the old quote, "When a student is ready, the teacher will appear" is true. I have found that a good counselor or mentor can be a great teacher. Counselors are sometimes able to bring to surface issues we have suppressed or not wanted to face. A powerful, effective counselor or coach will lead you to your inner power. They will guide you on your path to find the answers that lie within. Eventually, you will gain emotional independence and find your own powerful voice without prolonged dependency on the counselor.

Abandonment was a complex issue pervading many areas of my life. Until I worked with this issue in counseling, I did not realize how great of an issue it was for me. I just assumed that I wanted to take care of myself because I wasn't sure anyone could really be there for me. Subconsciously, I had decided I was the only one I could count on. So I mapped out my life at an early age in an effort to avoid the pain I had in childhood. I simply kept pressing on. I was a class clown in my early high school years, and totally out of touch with the depth of my pain. When I moved from one foster home to another one and changed high schools, the teachers who signed the transfer document were shocked that I was in foster care. I had not shown the signs of being a foster child. Then, when I left my marriage, my issues came crashing down around me.

Counseling assisted me in making major strides in personal development, and in opening to my Divine Inner Power. I have worked with three great professional teachers. My first counseling experience was with a pastoral counselor during my marriage separation. He was compassionate, wise, and to the point. We worked on my abandonment issues with my biological parents, issues I hadn't

Reinforcement Tools: Connecting With Your Divine Inner Power

consciously realized or confronted. His patience and understanding made a difference in my life. He helped me get in touch with what I felt and did not allow me to simply intellectualize my pain. This process was not an overnight cure, but a gradual process that was a great help. This counseling experience established a solid foundation for furthering my emotional development.

After working with the pastoral counselor, I met the counselor mentioned in Chapter One. She and I have worked on the processes of taking back my power and creating the life I desire. This experience opened a whole new world for me. We have worked with guided visualizations, affirmations, and meditation techniques. She also provided direct counseling and guidance. She is spiritually evolved and quite a teacher. Even her voice is melodic. I have made great changes in my life through our work together. She believes in me and my dreams, and supports my direction without forcing her ideas. My work with her continues as she gently helps to guide me in creating my own reality and looking within for my highest truths.

Another teacher I have worked with has helped me learn new techniques and processes of healing past wounds. My medical doctor referred me to a psychotherapist/energy healer for chronic neck pain. I had sought relief from my excruciating pain through various therapeutic methods and medications. After many failed attempts, I thought energy healing and chakra balancing work would at least be interesting. Somewhat reluctant, I went to see her. She administered the energy work and I found it very pleasant. More importantly, it actually helped with the pain for a few days. But, even more than that, it has helped me process emotional pain, which lifted slowly but surely. She also introduced me to the revolutionary EMDR — Eye Movement Desensitization & Reprocessing technique. EMDR is effective when used to eliminate or minimize symptoms associated with trauma, negative experiences, grief, and phobias. It is also helpful in rebuilding a healthy self-esteem. I strongly recommend this technique for processing and releasing major trauma issues. I was able to focus with great clarity during the EMDR sessions and release tremendous emotional pain. EMDR helped me heal the wound of leaving my first foster home and achieve mental clarity on writing. After one session, for example, I realized that my employer was not responsible for standing up for me. I was. I realized that I would not let anyone treat my dogs the way I was being treated, so why not stand up for me? And I did. Energy healing has helped me achieve greater emotional balance and served as a catalyst on my spiritual journey.

As you can see from my experience with mentors and counselors, this process is a valuable component of opening to your Divine Inner Power.

In his book, *The Road Less Traveled*, M. Scott Peck acknowledges the process of entering and committing to counseling is a courageous adventure. It is. It takes courage to be willing to face up to what is at the root of your unhappiness, and assume the responsibility to change your life. Assuming responsibility demonstrates your life is important, and is necessary to achieve real progress. Not assuming responsibility leaves you in the vulnerable position of victim or martyr, both of which leave you helpless. These roles involve thinking someone else is to blame for your unhappiness. Maybe

Reinforcement Tools: Connecting With Your Divine Inner Power

someone hurt you long ago, and this pain keeps you stuck, or perhaps you are in situation that you want to change or leave, but it is too frightening to think that you could be rejected or out there on your own. Thus, you surrender your power to live a joyful life. Why not decide that this is your life and living it fully is your choice?

Utilizing all of the powers available to you helps you on your journey to clear old programming and connect with the new rejuvenating energy. Reading, studying, attending functions with people of like minds, and connecting with a mentor or counselor can take you quite a distance on your path of connecting to your Divine Inner Power. These paths support, nurture, and promote your growth.

Take a step on your path and find inspiration through these words in St. Luke 12:30-31 —

For all these things do the nations of the world seek after; and your Father knoweth that ye have need of these things. But rather seek ye the kingdom of God; and all these things shall be added unto you.

Pursue the journey of looking inside — examine your life, for the kingdom of God is within you. The great philosopher Socrates, as he was facing death said —

I do nothing but go about persuading you all, old and young alike, not to take thought for your persons or your properties, but and chiefly to care about the greatest improvement of the soul. I tell you that virtue is not given by money, but that from virtue comes money and every other good of man, public as well as private.

The Divine Declaration

The Divine Declaration X – Reinforcement in Awakening To and Connecting With My Divine Inner Power

When in the course of my life, I find repression, unhappiness, ill-health, a chaotic state of mind, and a general sense of hopelessness, it is essential that I release any old programming, ties to the past, current situations, or people who are not supportive of my happiness, my ability to pursue my dreams, my general well-being, and my spiritual, emotional, and mental growth. I now assume my connection to God, the Divine Source, and recognize the power residing inside of me. I was created by the Divine Source; therefore, it must hold true that I am connected to this divinity and have access to a greater power. It is inside of me. It is my divine inheritance. I choose a new path of freedom from the albatross of unworthiness today. The weight is gone. A new world awaits me. And, so it is.

Thank you, Universe. Thank you, God.

Reinforcement Tools: Connecting With Your Divine Inner Power

I now accept as true and hold these truths to be evident: I now choose to open to my divinity, divine connection, and inner power. It is with courage and commitment that I fervently pursue this path. I know that taking the steps on the path of awakening are the steps to a better life. I know this is a path of my highest good. I am willing to take the steps that lead to my freedom, happiness, health, abundance, and joy. I will love myself on this journey. I am worthy, I am loved, I am loving, and I am love. I will listen to my inner guidance which will lead me and direct my way. Each time I listen to my inner voice, it becomes easier and easier to hear. My inner life creates my outer life. I know that like attracts like; therefore, I will work to become that which I wish to attract. There are various paths to the top of the mountain. I will choose my own path, listen to what resonates within me, and leave the rest. My path is lighted, and I travel with the understanding that God and the Universe support me on my journey. I am divine, and it is within my power to create the life I wish for. I am creating that life now.

My dreams are within reach. My life is getting better and better every day!

This is my Divine Declaration.

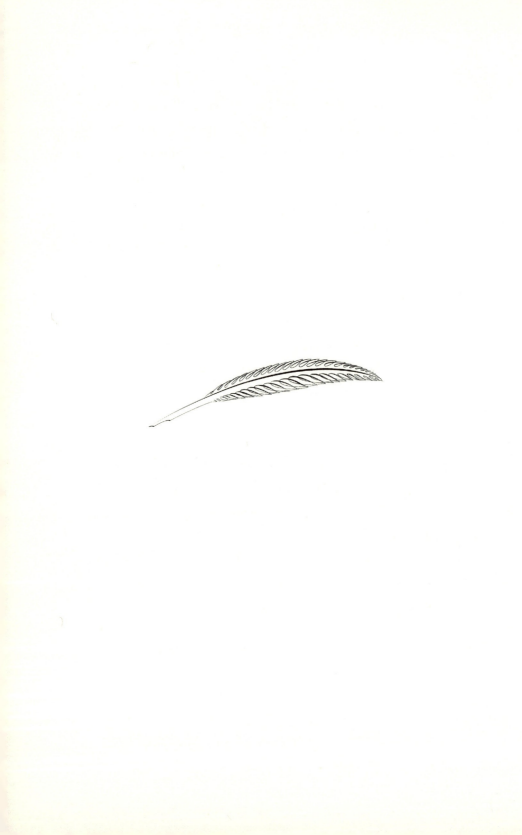

Chapter Eleven

Stand Tall, Live Authentically, Set Personal Boundaries and Enjoy Living in Your Divine Inner Power

The Divine Declaration

"Then, having done all, stand!"
— Annalee Skarin from Ephesians 6:13

"It was by learning internal boundaries that I could begin to achieve some integration and balance in my life, and transform my experience of life into an adventure that is enjoyable and exciting most of the time."
— Robert Burney

"I cannot believe that the inscrutable universe turns on an axis of suffering; surely the strange beauty of the world must somewhere rest on pure joy!"
— Louise Bogan

Stand Tall and Enjoy Living in Your Divine Inner Power

Your body language reveals your internal belief system. Your subconscious or subjective mind projects to others through your somatic (body or non-verbal) signals. Our verbal language reflects our cognitive processes when we speak. We also receive audible signals making sense of the verbal experience. Our somatic language is comprised of our physical signals. We send out somatic signals and receive signals from others. For instance, if we view something that generates fear or face a stressful moment, we may feel our chest tighten and an adrenaline rush, or we may experience fight-or-flight. We often respond to disappointment or sadness with our heads hung low and a somber countenance. We notice our body is more relaxed and open during times of joy and excitement than when we are under stress. Our face shows excitement, and our eyes light up when we are excited or happy. We smile, and can hardly contain the emotions within the boundaries of our physical body. If we have experienced prolonged physical or emotional abuse, we may have slouched shoulders that serve to protect us. If we feel inferior, we appear to carry the weight of the world on our shoulders, but when we feel confident, we stand tall and hold our heads high.

Furthermore, our bodies automatically respond to our environment. If we are cold, our pores close, and we shiver. When we are hot, our pores open, and we sweat. If we touch something too hot, we immediately withdraw from the heat. When we have a cold or an infection, our immune systems activate to eliminate the problem. We do not need to contemplate digesting our food, telling our hearts to beat, or our lungs to breathe, because these subconscious processes are automatic.

To become more aware of our non-verbal cues and to interpret signals from others, we need to take note of our own somatic postures. Take a moment to examine your somatic postures. Are you standing straight and tall with your head high? Are you able to look others in the eye when conversing with them? Do you cross your arms during a perceived threatening encounter? Do you use hand gestures, or do you restrain your body movement? Do you smile often, or do you frown much of the time? Do you clench your jaws or grind your teeth? Are your shoulders slumped and weighted with a heavy burden?

Some interpretations of our somatic language include the following:

Non-verbal Posture	**Signal Interpretation**
Erect posture, brisk walk	Confidence
Maintaining eye contact	Confidence and interest
Standing with hands on hips	Aggression or assertiveness
Legs crossed with swinging foot	Boredom
Sitting relaxed, with legs apart	Open and relaxed
Arms crossed on chest	Defensive

Stand Tall and Enjoy Living in Your Divine Inner Power

Walking with hands in pockets and shoulders slouched	Dejected or Disappointed
Cheek resting in hand	Pensive and evaluating
Rubbing hands together	Anticipation or excitement
Hands clasped behind head with legs crossed or propped up	Confidence or superiority
Hands clasped behind back	Open, confident, able to handle things
Open palm	Sincere, open, and innocent
Tapping fingers	Impatient
Patting or playing with hair	Lack of self-confidence or insecurity
Head tilted	Interested
Head straight	Authoritative
Nail biting	Insecure or nervous
Pulling on ear	Unsure
Clenched jaw	Anger
Jittery movements	Insecure or nervous
Eyes squinted or piercing look	Anger
Standing, shifting from side to side	Insecure, bored, or nervous
Maintaining eye contact	Interested and respectful
Body angled toward person	Attraction, interest, friendly
Body angled away from person	Dislike or disapproval
Pacing	Nervous
Smiling sheepishly with face down, eyes looking up	Flirting
Two people gazing across a room at each other	Romantic interest
Hand waving	Greeting or summoning

The Divine Declaration

These are some of the somatic signals we project and receive in our daily activities. Notice how your somatic signals differ when you interact in a professional environment than when you interact with friends and family. Your posture is likely more formal and reserved with professional peers than with those whom you share a close and comfortable relationship.

Connecting with your Divine Inner Power and understanding you are worthy changes your physical form. You stand taller and smile more often when you feel worthy and loved than when you feel rejected. Your belief that you deserve the best is displayed outwardly in your posture and behavior. You reveal confidence and steadfastness as you connect with your personal power. With confidence firmly placed in your inner power, it's difficult for others or circumstances to topple you. You stand tall and take the blows, becoming stronger for the experience. Much like gold is heated into existence, or steel is made stronger, you are tempered and grow stronger with each adversity you overcome. Soon you find that you can ignore and actually have sympathy for those who smite or use you because you understand their behavior is rooted in insecurity.

Your new energy attracts those who encourage you and are confident in their own skin — those who extend kindness and support to their fellow travelers. This kindness and support is their mark. You recognize people who are in touch with their inner power by their kindness, compassion, interest in others, ability to extend genuine compliments, and who also support others on their path. These people are the preferred kind of company. They do not passively agree, they genuinely support you. They have their own belief systems and they are happy to share with you and with the world.

As you progress on this path, you may even change your wardrobe. During a time when I was emotionally closed, I also dressed in a closed, conservative manner. I buttoned my blouses to the top, and accented with a scarf to seal securely the closed system that I covered with jackets to further protect my emotional vulnerability. I looked professional, but very stuffy. Then as I opened emotionally, I noticed my wardrobe became more flowing, feminine, and interesting.

Most of us have a style of dressing reflective of our inner values and our emotional state. Some men wear bow ties, some dress in western wear, and some don jackets or polo shirts. Women may have wardrobes consisting of mostly two piece suits, flowing feminine clothing, short skirts and low-cut blouses or bell-bottom jeans and T-shirts. Some of us may mix these styles to fit our mood. The "Dress for Success" era is actually on target. For those who want to belong to a certain group, your dress can take you a step closer to fitting in. Conversely, for those of you with a unique style, it may spur others to respect you for your individuality and creativity.

LIVE AUTHENTICALLY, SET PERSONAL BOUNDARIES, AND ENJOY THE REWARDS OF LIVING IN YOUR DIVINE INNER POWER

You are more powerful when you live in your "authentic *Self.*" This term means being who you truly are spiritually, and in all other aspects of your life. Don't try to be someone you're not to impress other people. Your authentic *Self* includes your personal preferences in your spiritual life, life purpose, relationships, hobbies and activi-

The Divine Declaration

ties, clothing, home, and all of the other things you choose for your life. When you free your authentic *Self*, you stand tall and hold your head high even when others' opinions and choices differ or conflict with your own. Commitment to living in your authenticity and connecting with your Divine Inner Power opens the space in which to manifest your ideal life.

You enjoy life more when you develop and live in your authenticity. This path is not a path of suffering and agony. Instead, it is one of understanding your divine connection and allowing your light to shine. You find yourself caring more about yourself, and taking time to allow for your growth and happiness.

Prior to this journey, you may have placed your wants and needs on the back burner as you handled others' requests or lived by someone else's standards. Helping others is admirable and wonderful, but if you subjugate your deepest desires and needs, this denial may lead to resentment and even physical illness. Remember to take care of you as you go about your life. Maintain a healthy balance of helping others and living in your authenticity.

To respect and honor our authentic selves, we must set personal boundaries. Our boundaries help define who we are and what we will and will not tolerate in our lives. Learning to set boundaries may feel uncomfortable at first, but the process becomes more natural to us as we move into living and honoring our genuine selves. We set boundaries with our professional peers, emotional boundaries in virtually all aspects of our lives, and spiritual boundaries as we embark on our spiritual journey.

Professionally, co-workers may encroach and cross over professional lines by making unwanted sexual advances, taking credit for your efforts, shifting their work responsibility to others in the office, being verbally disrespectful, or demonstrating their narcissistic behavior (A narcissist operates with the notion that other people exist only for his or her use or egotistical support). When people do not respect your boundaries, it is your chance to stand tall and seek a solution. Live in your power and don't allow the office politics or others' insecurities to negatively affect you. If someone crosses your emotional boundaries, you may choose to address the issue outright and work toward a mutual understanding and solution. You might also find removing yourself from a toxic environment is necessary. Take time to define your boundaries and seek a solution that allows you to maintain self-respect and live authentically.

Emotional boundaries involve consciously taking care of your emotional health, which also affects your physical health. In his book, *When the Body Says No*, Gabor Maté explains that people who put their emotional health on the back burner and spend their time catering to others often develop serious physical illnesses. Their body is saying "no" while they strive to please others. He tells us that if we must choose between guilt and resentment, guilt is the better choice. In other words, if you want to help someone say "yes," but if you prefer not to help, it is better to say no than to agree and become resentful as a result. Knowing your personal choice, and when to say yes or no, is the essence of setting emotional boundaries. For example, if someone demands your time or energy and you do not wish to participate, say "no" and if you choose, explain why. Causing a major confrontation isn't usually necessary.

The Divine Declaration

Many times we assume the role and serve in the capacity of a professional counselor to our friends and family members. It emotionally drains both the person serving as a counselor and the person seeking advice to maintain the rigorous, continual mock counseling sessions. Set your emotional boundaries, and return their life responsibilities back to them. Show them that they have their own inner power. If they need professional counseling, encourage them. They must decide to work on the issue, rather than plowing over the same ground with family and friends. You help them and yourself when you set boundaries.

Set boundaries financially as well. Helping someone financially can be a generous, but precarious proposition. Making sure that the terms and conditions are clear is an important element of financial generosity. Your boundaries may include a repayment schedule, or you may simply choose to give the money as a gift. Either is fine, but ensure the conditions are clear and acceptable for everyone involved. Helping others financially generates emotional stress if you expect repayment and the recipient doesn't repay the loan. If the payment arrangement works out exactly as planned, you will understand the value of stating clear terms. If the loan isn't repaid, you will likely be more careful about future lending. In either scenario, you learn the importance of setting boundaries. Helping out is wonderful when you can, but not if it is emotionally harmful for you.

Various situations require us to set emotional boundaries. We usually receive warning signals. We may distance ourselves from someone who is abrasive. We may prefer not to spend our energy on someone who does not live up to his or her word. If we notice

Stand Tall and Enjoy Living in Your Divine Inner Power

someone is undermining us or putting us down, we may emotionally need to move completely away from the individual.

Living in your truth is key to maintaining a healthy balance and standing tall in your power. Keeping pace with your soul's longings and helping others on their paths is part of an invigorating lifestyle. You are your caretaker on this journey. Don't allow others to take advantage of you, treat you with disregard, or demean you. If you maintain healthy emotional balance, you are taking a giant step on the path to your power. You gain great strength in your emotions and mental health each time you stand up for yourself and protect your emotional well-being.

Your spiritual boundaries help define your soul's growth. As you pursue your spiritual journey, you will know your truth in your heart. Love, kindness, generosity, and healthy support for your fellow travelers become part of your life as you experience your inner power, joy, and peace. Setting boundaries in your spiritual life includes making time to pray and meditate, getting involved with causes that are dear to your heart, cultivating your divine relationship with God or Divine Source, and living fully in your truth. While some people may not align with your spiritual path, remember we all seek the same light as we travel through this lifetime. Some travelers choose lessons of great agony, drama, and grief while others choose to learn through bliss and expansion. We learn many lessons as our soul develops and we awaken to our divine connection.

Living in your authenticity creates forward momentum for creating your ideal life, and provides greater understanding concerning why you deserve happiness and success. Your life prefer-

The Divine Declaration

ences rise to the surface as you open to your authentic *Self*. Your ideal life may include your career or life's purpose, a divine right partner, having children or pets, or finding the perfect place to live. Is your ideal home setting in a rural area, by a meadow, by the ocean, in the desert, or in the city? Take time to feel your ideal life. Can you see the flowers in the meadow, hear the ocean roaring, feel the hot dry desert air, or envision the hustle and bustle of the city? Do you smile when you focus and visualize this ideal life? Explore these questions with excitement and the expectation of your highest good manifesting in ways even greater than you imagine.

Take time to know your dreams and realize your potential. Connect with your Divine Inner Power and experience lasting joy and peace. You will face many of your challenges with "ease and grace" when you walk this powerful inner path. When grief or despair surface, you now have a deep, abiding, divine connection to provide you strength. Daily challenges with your finances, health, relationships, or career are easier now that you have this connection to help you discover workable solutions. The peace of knowing your eternal, divine spiritual nature brings you renewed strength and fortitude. Your life takes on a different meaning when experienced from this grounded foundation of inner power.

Stand tall and hold your head high. Live authentically and know that you deserve happiness and success. You are a child of God, a spark of the Divine. You are here to develop the beautiful spirit of you and manifest your divine glory. Reveal your light as you acknowledge the light of others on their paths, spend time connecting with your Divine Inner Power, express your love without

Stand Tall and Enjoy Living in Your Divine Inner Power

reservation, encourage someone who needs a helping hand, take time to enjoy the things in your life for which you are grateful, forgive someone, use discernment and set healthy boundaries, live up to your potential, smile, speak a kind word to someone in need, take a stand for a worthy cause, wear the old shirt you love that may be out of style, stay determined in the face of adversity, enjoy nature, take a needed vacation, gaze at the stars, speak up for yourself, move toward supportive people in your life, release unhealthy relationships, learn something new, take time out for a hobby, listen to uplifting music, dance the blues away, and reach the heartfelt understanding that you have great value and declare your divine connection!

The Divine Declaration

The Divine Declaration XI – Stand Tall, Live Authentically, Set Boundaries, and Enjoy Living in Your Divine Inner Power

When in the course of my life, I find repression, unhappiness, ill-health, a chaotic state of mind, and a general sense of hopelessness, it is essential that I release any old programming, ties to the past, current situations, or people who are not supportive of my happiness, my ability to pursue my dreams, my general well-being and my spiritual, emotional and mental growth. I now assume my connection to God, the Divine Source, and recognize the power residing inside of me. I was created by the Divine Source; therefore, it must hold true that I am connected to this divinity and have access to a greater power. It is inside of me. It is my divine inheritance. I choose a new path of freedom from the albatross of unworthiness today. The weight is gone. A new world awaits me. And, so it is.

Thank you, Universe. Thank you, God.

Stand Tall and Enjoy Living in Your Divine Inner Power

I now accept as true and hold these truths to be evident: Today I stand tall. I have prepared for this day. I am true to myself and my beliefs. I set personal boundaries and feel confident in my decisions. I am now able to make decisions to move forward in the direction of my dreams. I know my thoughts create, and I am careful what I feed my mind. I nourish my life through practicing positive thinking, meditating, praying, communing with nature, attentive focus, and living in my truth. I enjoy my family and friends as I accept our differences and celebrate our common ground. I allow others to pursue their paths as I pursue my path to the light. I release negative energy, unsupportive people, and personal grudges. This new space is filled with creative energy. I use this energy to create the life I really want to live. I spend time connecting with my dreams. I open to my highest good and to the highest good of all. I allow divine energy to flow into my life and allow it to flow outward as I share with others. I am building a life of harmony, peace, love, abundance, and greater well-being. Today I take one more step forward on this extraordinary journey toward the beautiful life awaiting me. I now choose to awaken to my divinity, lovability, and I declare my divine connection to God, the Source, and All That Is — my life depends on it.

This is my Divine Declaration.

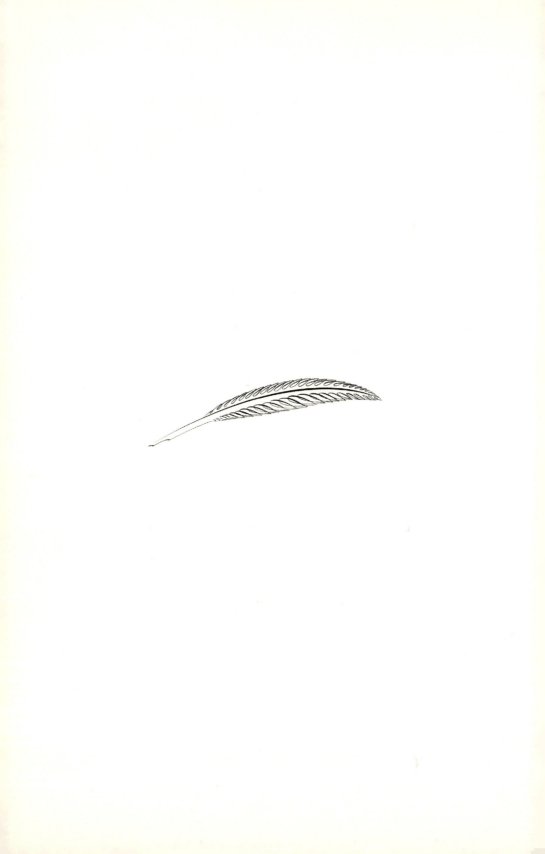

Chapter Twelve

The Divine Declaration

The Divine Declaration

"Your vision will become clear when you can look into your own heart. Who looks outside, dreams; who looks inside, awakens."
– Carl Jung

The Divine Declaration

When in the course of my life, I find repression, unhappiness, ill-health, a chaotic state of mind, and a general sense of hopelessness, it is essential that I release any old programming, ties to the past, current situations, or people who are not supportive of my happiness, my ability to pursue my dreams, my general well-being, and my spiritual, emotional, and mental growth.

I now assume my connection to God, the Divine Source, and recognize the power residing inside of me. I was created by the Divine Source; therefore, it must hold true that I am connected to this divinity and have access to a greater power. It is inside of me. It is my divine inheritance. I choose a new path of freedom from the albatross of unworthiness today. The weight is gone. A new world awaits me. And, so it is.

Thank you, Universe. Thank you, God.

The Divine Declaration

I – UNDERSTANDING MY DIVINITY AND POWER

I now accept as true and hold these truths to be evident: I am a divine being, a spark of the Divine Source. I am worthy. I am loving and loved. I live in a supportive world, supported by God, the Divine Source. My inheritance is abundance in love, health, joy, peace, and all my heart desires for a wonderful life. I know that I deserve the best in life and it is mine. All I need to do is to awaken to this truth. My divine power is available anytime I choose to use it. It is always there and serves as a beacon guiding me on the path of my highest good. I fulfill my dreams and live in the abundance and joy that it is mine. My life is a work in progress. I am on my path of love and light. I am excited about the future, able to let go of the past and find peace in the present moment. With great fortitude, I embark on this journey of light. My divine connection is infinite, and my divine power is unlimited. I can soar. I have the ability to make my dreams come true.

Today, I declare my divinity and access my power with courage and commitment.

This is my Divine Declaration.

II – RELEASING RESISTANCE TO MY DIVINITY AND DIVINE POWER

I now accept as true and hold these truths to be evident: I choose my world today. I will be courageous and deal with my fears directly. I know in my heart that the Divine Source wants my best; therefore, there is only hope. The fear that is paralyzing my life and delaying my dreams is an imaginary obstacle in my life, something that I can remove by changing my view of the fear. I choose to face the fear, do whatever it takes to let go of it, and take back my power. My self-esteem is critical to my success and happiness. It is my gauge of how I treat myself. I am worthy, and, regardless of past circumstances, I have great value. I love myself more and more each day. I see the little child in me, and I nurture that child with love, respect, and emotional support. I forgive myself for past mistakes and forgive others who may have hurt me intentionally or unintentionally. It is for my own sake that I release this old tattered pain of the past. I determine my own worth based on my own value system. I know that I am a child of God, and the child part of me that was hurt is also a child of God. I live acknowledging my divine inheritance. I know that I have worth. I move forward in life, decide the life I want, and take the steps to manifest my dreams. My life choices now belong to me. There is no one to blame. I am strong. I am powerful. I am divine. It is through this divine connection that I fly from the nest to live my dreams. There is nothing to fear. I am worthy and powerful, and the past is healed.

The future is bright for me. My present thoughts are creating my life from this day forward. My highest good is manifesting in greater ways than I even imagined.

This is my Divine Declaration.

III – MY THOUGHTS ARE CREATING MY LIFE

I now accept as true and hold these truths to be evident: I live in the divine light because I am a part of God or All That Is. I am in divine guidance each and every day. Everything I do and say is divinely guided. My thoughts are creating my experience. I believe the truth of my divine connection to God and universal power is the real me. Therefore, I am always connected to my divinity, love, and life expression. I can believe in my good and I do. My highest good is always available. I allow it into my experience now. When I tune into my divine power, I create the life I want to live. I create the form for my life through my conscious thoughts, fill it with the substance through my feelings of faith and enthusiasm, and experience my highest good in the physical realm. I live in universal abundance, health, happiness, peace, and love. Because I know that all knowledge is available to me if I allow it to enter into my space, I seek and find the answers to my life challenges. I know that I know that I know. The universal abundance is mine and available to me this very moment.

This is my Divine Declaration.

IV – MY HEALTHY MIND, BODY, AND SPIRIT

I now accept as true and hold these truths to be evident: My emotional and spiritual thoughts are contributing to my physical health. I find it appealing to eat healthy foods. I choose an exercise I enjoy and make it a consistent part of my life. I take charge of my own health and make choices that reflect my inner power. I release any guilt surrounding my physical health. I know that my emotions affect my health and guilt has no place here. It is with a sense of healing power that I assume responsibility for my health. I will now pursue the route of spiritual, emotional and physical health. I am excited about moving forward in a direction that promotes my well-being. I will work to release any anger or fear I am holding as this release will free energy for a more positive outlook on life. I will work to resolve any situations in my life that are emotionally intolerable. I will take the steps in my life to know who I really am and explore my options to live up to my dreams and potential. I take this opportunity to heal my life and I willingly go forth to experience my spiritual, emotional, and physical well-being.

This is my Divine Declaration.

V – EXPERIENCING AND EXPANDING MY DIVINE INNER POWER

I now accept as true and hold these truths to be evident: I am in charge of my life. Beginning today, I will do the things that will elevate my life. I will do at least one thing that is encouraging and inspirational. I am in awe of the universal abundance that surrounds me. I am an heir to this abundance. I need not fret or manipulate, nor become anxious about where or how my abundance will take form. I need only to connect with the Divine Source and know what I want for my life. It is through this divine connection that I access my abundance. My divine inner power will direct me toward my dreams. I will listen and take the steps toward greater fulfillment. I will spend time connecting to my divinity and strengthening my divine inner power. I pursue my dreams with excitement and take time to bring them to fruition. As I develop and connect with the real me, my life changes in positive ways. I am able to focus on what I want in life and take the steps to make it happen. I know it is up to me. I will love myself on this journey. I am worthy, I am loved, I am loving, and I am love.

This is my Divine Declaration.

VI – SUPPORT FOR MY LIFE GROWTH AND DREAMS

I now accept as true and hold these truths to be evident: I will build my support system. My internal support system, my connection with my Divine Inner Power, is quite powerful. It is important that I surround myself with people who support me. I release anyone who is hindering my spiritual growth and personal development. To live my dreams, I must look upward toward the open sky and keep my vision ahead. It is no longer necessary to keep the company of people who interfere with this vision. I let go of the naysayers and bless them out of my life. My life is on track with my highest good, and I fill my life with people who support my highest good. I also support them on their journey to live their dreams. We share a mutual trust and encourage happiness, health, and abundance. I find greater support as I connect with my Divine Inner Power. This power is operating in my life always. I know I am a divine spark of God, the Divine Source, and this connection provides me great strength and determination.

This is my Divine Declaration.

VII – LOVE, GRATITUDE, AND FORGIVENESS

I now accept as true and hold these truths to be evident: I now understand that I must love my Self in order to really be capable of loving another. It is through understanding I am a spark of the Divine Source that I am able to tap into my Divine Inner Power and learn to love me. I am love, loving, loved, and lovable. I am grateful that I now know these valuable truths about my Self. I spend time each day remembering my value. If I am in touch with my divinity, I see the divinity in others. I start each day with gratitude. I find at least one thing for which I am grateful every day. My gratitude expands and opens my life to more wonderful things daily. I can forgive others who may have hurt me along the way. It is for me that I work on forgiveness. I now know that when I forgive someone, I free myself from the bondage of pain. I release my Self from this pain. It is clear that loving me, focusing on things for which I am grateful, and forgiving past hurts releases me to live the divine life I deserve.

This is my Divine Declaration.

VIII – DISCOVERING AND PURSUING MY DIVINE RIGHT LIVELIHOOD

I now accept as true and hold these truths to be evident: I have decided to pursue my dreams. I take this step forward. I see others who are successful and know that I can be successful, too. I know many people live their dreams and knowing this reinforces my belief in my own ability. I have people in my life who support me on my divine right livelihood path. It is with determination and energy I move forward to live the life I deserve, a life of joy, abundance, and love. I am aligned with my life purpose and find direction with every step I take. I am excited and see myself as successful and fulfilling my purpose daily. My Divine Right Livelihood is a great part of my journey and I know I have every opportunity to succeed. Love lights the way, joy greets me on my path, and harmony and abundance manifest in all areas of my life. I have hope and faith in my journey now. I find greater confidence and fortitude as I handle each challenge with ease and grace. I share the joy of others as they also pursue their dreams.

This is my Divine Declaration.

IX – OPENING TO THE FLOW OF THE UNIVERSE AND SHARING

I now accept as true and hold these truths to be evident: I am open to the abundance of the universe. I open my heart, soul, and mind to all the good things that I am attracting into my life. I know that God is infinite and universal supply is abundant and infinite. I allow wonderful adventures, beautiful relationships, a healthy body and mind, and abundant resources and means to fulfill my divine right path in life. I open to sharing my life with others. Opening to the abundance of the universe is allowance. Sharing is the outflow, creating space for new expansive energy into my life. It is the cycle of universal abundance. I receive, give, and receive again. I create a continual cycle of blessings in my life and in the lives of others through sharing. I release the old and open to the new. With enthusiasm, I allow the power of the universe into my life! Infinite love encircles me and permeates every aspect of my life. Love and light-guide my unfolding path day by day. I am more peaceful as I trust divine love. Support accompanies me on my journey every step of the way. I know my highest good is in divine order as well as the highest good of all. I remain true to my authentic Self on this journey. I am open and loving. From my internal center of love and light, I send love and light out to the universe.

This is my Divine Declaration.

X – REINFORCEMENT IN AWAKENING TO AND CONNECTING WITH MY DIVINE INNER POWER

I now accept as true and hold these truths to be evident: I now choose to open to my divinity, divine connection, and inner power. It is with courage and commitment that I fervently pursue this path. I know that taking the steps on the path of awakening are the steps to a better life. I know this is a path of my highest good. I am willing to take the steps that lead to my freedom, happiness, health, abundance, and joy. I will love myself on this journey. I am worthy, I am loved, I am loving, and I am love. I will listen to my inner guidance which will lead me and direct my way. Each time I listen to my inner voice, it becomes easier and easier to hear. My inner life creates my outer life. I know that like attracts like; therefore, I will work to become that which I wish to attract. There are various paths to the top of the mountain. I will choose my own path, listen to what resonates within me, and leave the rest. My path is lighted, and I travel with the understanding that God and the Universe support me on my journey. I am divine, and it is within my power to create the life I wish for. I am creating that life now. My dreams are within reach. My life is getting better and better every day!

This is my Divine Declaration.

XI – STAND TALL, LIVE AUTHENTICALLY, SET BOUNDARIES, AND ENJOY LIVING IN YOUR DIVINE INNER POWER

I now accept as true and hold these truths to be evident: Today I stand tall. I have prepared for this day. I am true to myself and my beliefs. I set personal boundaries and feel confident in my decisions. I am now able to make decisions to move forward in the direction of my dreams. I know my thoughts create, and I am careful what I feed my mind. I nourish my life through practicing positive thinking, meditating, praying, communing with nature, attentive focus, and living in my truth. I enjoy my family and friends as I accept our differences and celebrate our common ground. I allow others to pursue their paths as I pursue my path to the light. I release negative energy, unsupportive people, and personal grudges. This new space is filled with creative energy. I use this energy to create the life I really want to live. I spend time connecting with my dreams. I open to my highest good and to the highest good of all. I allow divine energy to flow into my life and allow it to flow outward as I share with others. I am building a life of harmony, peace, love, abundance, and greater well-being. Today I take one more step forward on this extraordinary journey toward the beautiful life awaiting me. I now choose to awaken to my divinity, lovability and I declare my divine connection to God, the Source and All That Is — my life depends on it.

This is my Divine Declaration.

Bibliography

Bach, Richard, and Leslie Parrish-Bach. *Illusions: The Adventures of a Reluctant Messiah.* New York: Dell, 1977

Bach, Richard. *Jonathan Livingston Seagull.* New York: HarperCollins, 1973

Brennan, Barbara Ann. *Light Emerging.* New York: Bantam, 1993

Chopra, Deepak, M.D. *Timeless Mind, Ageless Body: The Quantum Alternative to Growing Old.* New York: Three Rivers Press, 1993

Chopra, Deepak, M.D. *Creating Affluence, The A-to-Z Steps to a Richer Life.* California: New World Library, 1998

Cole-Whittaker, Terry. *What You Think of Me is None of My Business.* New York: Jove, 1979

Diamond, Harvey and Marilyn. *Fit for Life.* New York: Warner, 1985

Gawain, Shakti. *Creative Visualization.* California: New World Library, 2002

Holmes, Ernest. *The Science of Mind.* New York: Jeremy P. Tarcher, 1938

Jeffers, Susan. *Feel the Fear and Do It Anyway.* New York: Ballantine, 1987

Jennings, Rev. Jesse, ed. *The Essential Ernest Holmes.* New York: Jeremy P. Tarcher/Putnam, 2002

Kelder, Peter. *Ancient Secrets of the Fountain of Youth.* New York: Doubleday, 1985

Maté, Gabor, M.D. *When the Body Says No.* New Jersey: John Wiley & Sons, 2003

Rand, Ayn. *Atlas Shrugged.* New York: Penguin Putnam, 1957, 1985, 1992

Rinpoche, Sogyal. *The Tibetan Book of Living and Dying.* New York: HarperCollins, 1993

Sarno, John, M.D. *The MindBody Prescription.* New York: Warner, 1998

Spalding, Baird. *Life and Teaching of the Masters of the Far East.* California: DeVorss, 1964

The King James Version *Holy Bible.* London: The University Press.

Weil, Andrew, M.D. *Spontaneous Healing.* New York: Ballantine, 1995

Williamson, Marianne. *A Return to Love.* New York: HarperCollins, 1992

Wart, Paula J. "Longevity May Have Spiritual Link" 2001: Online Wellness Center, Vanderbilt University Health Plus Wellness program. http://vanderbilt.owc.wellsource.com

Excerpt from *Mind/Body Connection: How Your Emotions Affect Your Health.* 2004: American Academy of Family Physicians. http://familydoctor.org/782.xml

Recommended Reading

Bennett, Hal Zina, and Susan T. Sparrow. *Follow Your Bliss.* California: Tenacity Press, 1997

Recommended Reading

Cherry, Joanna. *Living Mastery*. California: Oughten House, 1998

Colbert, Don, M.D. *Deadly Emotions*. Tennessee: Thomas Nelson, 2003

Dyer, Wayne. *You'll See It When You Believe It*. New York: HarperCollins, 1989

Dyer, Wayne. *Manifest Your Destiny*. New York: HarperPaperbacks, 1997

Dyer, Wayne. *The Power of Intention*. California: Hay House, 2004

Emerson, Ralph Waldo. *The Selected Writings of Ralph Waldo Emerson*. New York: Penguin, 1965

Gibran, Kahlil. *The Prophet*. New York: Knopf, 1923

Harricharan, John. *When You Can Walk on Water, Take the Boat*. Georgia: New World, 1986, 1999

Harricharan, John. *Morning Has Been All Night Coming*. Georgia: New World, 1991

Mandino, Og. *The Greatest Miracle in the World*. Florida: Frederick Fell, 1975

Murphy, Joseph. *The Power of Your Subconscious Mind*. New York: Bantam, 2000

Schucman, Helen and William Thetford. *A Course in Miracles*. California: Foundation for Inner Peace, 1975, 1985, 1992

Skarin, Analee. *Ye Are Gods*. California: DeVorss, 1952, 1979

The Divine Declaration

About the Author

Jane brings unique perspective and dedication to her writing. She grew up in the state foster care system. Having grown up in this system, she learned about self-reliance, emotional resilience and personal power at an early age. With steadfast perseverance and determination, she triumphed over the odds and statistics. She graduated with a Bachelor of Arts Degree in Psychology from Oglethorpe University in Atlanta, Georgia. Human behavior, motivation and spirituality have been the central focus of her education and life experience for twenty years. She has studied both areas academically and experientially. She has published motivational articles in several newsletters and an industry newspaper. She has also written and implemented corporate promotional campaigns for a statewide business publication and for publishing support companies. Jane has achieved professional success in the areas of accounting, management, marketing and sales. Her story is one of overcoming adversity, staying the course and living her dreams. She is passionate about helping others realize their potential. She also loves animals and is concerned with their well-being and humane treatment.